MW00653758

"In *Register Your Book,* ... case for something tha... publishing for a while... book—and doing it properly—is vital to your success as an author. Then he proceeds to break down this often-confusing process in bite-size pieces that even the least publishing-savvy reader will have no difficulty following along with. Straightforward and easy to digest, this is one how-to that every new author or publisher should have in their arsenal!"

> —*Brooke Warner, Publisher of She Writes Press and author of* Green-Light Your Book: How Writers Can Succeed in the New Era of Publishing

"An essential guide to publishing identifiers, their benefits and uses, and (most importantly) what NOT to do. Required reading for every new entrant into book publishing—and for those who have been here a while, it's never too late to go back to the sound fundamentals that David Wogahn provides here."

> —*Laura Dawson, Numerical Gurus*

"Does your head hurt from hunting for answers for all of those pesky little questions you have about ISBNs, bar codes, copyright, and library registration? David Wogahn has been my go-to guy for answers on this topic for years now, and I'm thrilled that he's provided this information in one concise guide. Keep it close and proceed with confidence in spending your time and dollars to get it done right, the first time."

> —*Carla King, Self-Pub Boot Camp*

"David Wogahn's book offers newly published authors and independent publishers a concise and clear guide to the prepublication process. Anyone looking for information on ISBNs, copyright, and a host of other details for independent publishing needs this book."

> —*Rachelle Yousuf, President, Women's National Book Association—Los Angeles Chapter*

"Where was David Wogahn when I was starting out in book publishing? The learning curve is so steep in this business. Not only do you need to know how to design, produce, promote, and distribute a book; you must also be an expert at what I'll call the 'minutia' of publishing. Sure, you could spend—and waste—dozens of hours figuring out how all this works. But why wouldn't you just read Wogahn's book?"
　　—*Wendy Thomas Russell,* Publisher and Co-Founder, Brown Paper Press

"It is true that almost anybody today can publish a book in whatever slap-dash fashion they wish. To my mind the test is in the quality of the details, language, and production. A book's public life begins with an ISBN. Wogahn's *Register Your Book* starts you off on the right road."
　　—*Mike Sager,* Editor & Publisher, The Sager Group LLC

"This book is a must-have for any author who is considering the self-publishing route. *Register Your Book* demystifies the confusing labyrinth of copyright registration, ISBN selection, and marketing your book to libraries. Highly recommended."
　　—*Christine Pinheiro,* President of Defiant Press

**REGISTER
YOUR BOOK**

Also by David Wogahn

My Publishing Imprint

The Book Review Companion

The Book Reviewer Yellow Pages, 9th Edition

Successful eBook Publishing

Marketing and Distributing eBooks
(LinkedIn Learning)

REGISTER YOUR BOOK

The Essential Guide to ISBNs, Barcodes, Copyright, and LCCNs

 DAVID WOGAHN

PartnerPress

Carlsbad, California

Register Your Book: The Essential Guide to ISBNs, Barcodes, Copyright, and LCCNs
Second Edition
© 2016-2019 David Wogahn, All Rights Reserved.

www.DavidWogahn.com

Available in these formats:
- 978-1-944098-11-7 (Paperback)
- 978-1-944098-06-3 (eBook)

Library of Congress Control Number: 2019944495

Editing: Katie Barry
Cover design: Anton Stefanov Rangelov
Publishing Services: Kerri Esten, AuthorImprints
Audiobook producer: Carter Wogahn

Published by PartnerPress | Carlsbad, California

For volume and resale pricing, please contact publish@partnerpress.org

It's the little details that are vital.
Little things make big things happen.

— John Wooden,
Legendary UCLA basketball coach

Contents

The Countdown to Book Launch™ Series

The Countdown to Book Launch series is for authors, self-publishers, and small presses with limited time and a need for authoritative publishing information informed by real-world experience. Each book focuses on its intended topic and avoids fluff or filler material.

The material presented in each book has been thoroughly researched and recommendations are made based on personal experience. But as it can be with how-to guides, information and resource links are subject to change over time. I help readers cope with this in two unique ways.

1. Hyperlinks to online references in each book are replaced with a URL link shortener domain: breve.link. It works like Bitly or TinyURL; long, complicated links are replaced with easy-to-read and maintain links. It allows us to keep the links

in your book working and makes it easier to look-up links if you are reading the paperback. More on this in the first chapter.

2. Members of my mailing list receive advance notice about exclusive launch offers when I release a book or training resource. Join my mailing list at:

DavidWogahn.com/join

or subscribe to one of the free resources at AuthorImprints.com to be notified.

> To your success,
> David Wogahn
>
> DavidWogahn.com
> AuthorImprints.com

Edition Highlights

The following is a brief summary of the major changes between this 2019 edition and the first edition released in 2016.

Chapter 2, International Standard Book Number (ISBN)

1. Amazon phased out CreateSpace and merged its print-on-demand (POD) functionality into KDP Print. Terminology and ISBN information was updated to reflect this.
2. Amazon also changed Expanded Distribution. Books are no longer required to use an Amazon ISBN to be included in an online catalog used by libraries and schools to order books.
3. A new sidebar was added to address the decision about what name to use when registering ISBNs.
4. MyIdentifiers no longer encourages publishers to upload a PDF of their book; in fact, they removed this optional feature entirely.

Chapter 3, Barcodes

KDP Print makes it clear you can upload a cover with a barcode that has a price. They also added a label to the cover that clearly indicates the paperback is a proof edition.

Chapter 4, Copyright

In 2019, the U.S. Supreme Court clarified when someone can sue for copyright violation. There is no change—your copyright still needs to be registered, not simply filed. I highlight this important fact in this chapter.

Chapter 5, Library of Congress

The Library replaced its antiquated online filing system with a modern interface. They also created a streamlined process for authors and self-publishers to request a Library of Congress Control Number (LCCN).

Other changes

1. I expanded the table of ISBN requirements by store to include all the eBook distributors (aggregators) referenced in my eBook Distributor Round-up for 2019.
2. All hyperlinks were verified.
3. The reported numbers about ISBN usage were updated.

Preface

Today's authors have a choice. In 2008, just 77,132 indie books were published. Ten years later in 2017, the most recent year data is available, more than one million self-published books were published[1]. Independent publishing is indeed a viable option. However, the greatest stumbling block that remains for most indie publishers is making sense of the registration process that enables the sale and protection of books.

That's where I can help you.

This guide will save you from sorting through blogs and message boards that contain contradictory statements and misinformed opinions. It will save you the heartache of launching a book without fully understanding the ramifications of your choices for assigning an ISBN or the proper elements of a copyright page and its filing. Finally, you can avoid wading through arcane government website pages to learn the requirements, process, and timing for obtaining a Library of Congress Control Number.

My goal is to simplify the publication process. Registration is one of the few steps in book publishing in which mistakes and oversights are difficult and costly to correct. These pages explain your options, advise possible courses of action, and help you avoid the consequences of actions not taken.

Register Your Book presents the essential information any United States–based publisher needs to succeed. Think of it as your personal publishing consultant.

1

What Book Registration Is and Why It Matters

Book registration in the United States is not a formal requirement, nor a defined procedure for every book. Anyone can print a book or produce an eBook and distribute it. You do not need to complete any paperwork or online forms, or spend any money. However, if you wish to distribute, sell, and protect your book, there are three separate registrations that all books have in common:

1. ISBN (International Standard Book Number) registration
2. U.S. copyright registration
3. U.S. Library of Congress registration

Who might be able to ignore these registrations? Perhaps the fiction writer publishing exclusively in eBook format who doesn't care about copyright. But for the vast majority of us who don't fit that description, one or more of these registrations is important, if not mandatory, for publishing a book.

Following the advice in this book, no one will be able to tell the difference between your book and a book produced by one of the "big New York" publishers. Besides simply *appearing* professional, your book can be:

- Listed in the same industry databases.
- Sold in any store that wishes to sell your book.
- More easily (and less expensively) be defended in the event of a copyright violation.

Your book will also be more *discoverable* by those looking for books like yours: stores, libraries, and, most importantly, readers. No matter how you describe it, in Internet marketing-speak, no book or author stands a chance at success without being visible and discoverable to readers searching online. And with more brick-and-mortar stores closing, book shoppers are making more of their purchases online.

Never before has there been a more compelling reason for making sure a book and its author are properly represented in as many online databases as possible. A thorough book registration process ensures that. Proper book registration will greatly reduce the chance of problems for many years to come.

Who this book is for

The ease of publishing and the potential for income from it have brought literally thousands of new books to the virtual shelves of online bookstores. R.R. Bowker, the exclusive source of ISBNs in the United States, reported in October 2018 that ISBNs assigned to self-published print books grew from 235,639 in 2012 to 879,587 in 2017, a 273% increase in five years(1). And as noted in the preface, the actual numbers are even greater when you include eBooks with an ISBN—a number that would be higher still if you counted eBooks published without an ISBN, a number that only Amazon knows.

That's because the big eBook retailers—Amazon, Apple, Barnes & Noble, Google, Kobo, and Smashwords—do not require publishers to use an ISBN. And because none of the large online self-publishing portals report the number of new eBooks published, no one knows just how many new eBooks are published each year without an ISBN. Suffice to say, it must be thousands.

Numbers and growth aside, what's obvious is that we have a highly competitive marketplace. This makes it especially important for new publishers to utilize every industry program and procedure available.

Register Your Book aims to assist the range of people seeking to navigate the complicated world of self-publishing:

- **Self-publishers** who want to avoid having their book *look* self-published and get it into the same catalogs and databases as the large publishers use
- **Authors** who want to understand their options even if they are not the one designing and producing their book
- **Publishing services firms** that want to help their clients look professional and guide them through these important steps
- **New publishers** who need to establish best practices that will serve their publishing firm for years to come

It doesn't matter, until it matters

We publish with the goal of being successful, whether that means selling books, touching lives, recording family histories, or enhancing our reputations. But all of that is put at risk when we take shortcuts or miss important details.

Publishing a book is a journey culminating in an event. Once released into the world, your book is on its own. Do-overs and corrections are expensive, if not impossible.

Consider ISBNs. Numbers cannot be transferred, so if you got a free one and later want to show your name as the publisher, you will have to re-publish your book using a new ISBN. And that may mean starting over to accumulate reader reviews.

You might discover a book similar to yours selling in the U.S. or another country, but now the cost to protect your copyright has ballooned from $35 to thousands of dollars.

Or—surprise—a chance media mention generates interest in your book, but libraries and schools can't easily find it. Because it is already published, your book is ineligible to receive a Library of Congress Control Number.

As publishers, we need to plan for success. Publishing a book is like baking a loaf of bread. Once out of the oven, the ingredients are baked in, and it's off to the shelf for sale. Your book's registration information never changes.

How to use this book

Register Your Book seeks to address both the *why* and *how* questions that new or occasional publishers have. If you are new to publishing, I recommend that you read the book but skim the how-to sections on your first time through. Don't get bogged down trying to complete each step of the process as you read it. Registering your book requires a good deal of thinking and decision-making, so it's best to understand the big picture before you get started.

After your initial read, turn to **Appendix A, Timing and Timelines**, where I summarize how long a process takes as well as the general order of each registration step. Each step references the appropriate chapter, which you can reread as you complete that step in the process.

Website links

Each step of the registration process is completed online, and that is where you will find all of the additional website resources referenced in this book. To make accessing these resources easier for both printed book and eBook readers, I replaced each of the specific links with an easy-to-read short link that takes you to the same place.

Each link begins with the domain name breve.link (*breve* means *short* in Italian). For example, when you type or click http://breve.link/ryb1, you will be taken to the Bowker website page for title submissions: http://www.bowker.com/tools-resources/Title-Submissions.html.

Not only does this make a long website address easier to read and type (especially helpful for print book readers), but, when an address changes, we can easily update the link to keep your book accurate and up-to-date. Please email the publisher (Publish@PartnerPress.org) if a link is broken or goes to what you think is the wrong location. That way it can be quickly fixed for all readers.

Book or eBook?

As you read on, keep in mind that I use the term *book* to describe all forms of a book—paper, digital, audio—unless referring specifically to the eBooks sold by major online book retailers. And by eBooks, I mean Kindle (sometimes called Mobi) and EPUB formats, not PDF or any of the other dozen or so eBook formats.[2]

My opinion is that we—as publishers—do our readers and profession a disservice if we treat eBooks as a second-class format. An eBook can and should be as professionally produced a work as any other type of book. We need to be careful that we don't create a lesser product in the minds of today's readers.

To this last point, if you are publishing books—whether the "p," the "e," or the "a" (audio) variety—and assigning them an ISBN, do it right. An ISBN is inherently helpful for sales, but only if you take advantage of everything it offers.

Let's begin with the most important registration step: the International Standard Book Number, or ISBN.

2

The International Standard Book Number

The International Standard Book Number (ISBN) has been a fixture in book retailing for more than 50 years. Its purpose is to identify a book with as much certainty as possible, which is no small feat when you consider all the different editions, formats, languages, and shapes a book can take.

It is like a serial number: every edition needs one. Once assigned, it never changes, even if the language, format, or content change. It matters to the entire book eco-system: search engines, libraries, bookstores, wholesalers, distributors, inventory, and sales software, and, ultimately, readers.

But a few curious things began to happen with the rise of digital media. For one thing, the book itself has morphed from its traditional container of paper into digital forms and formats such as CD-ROM, Mobi, EPUB, MP3, and PDF. These developments have enabled publishers to offer enhancements such as video and hyperlinks to external resources. No doubt this has become the source of the mythical eISBN,[3] a term that has no meaning or basis.

Up until the introduction of the Kindle and EPUB eBook file formats, the rules for ISBN use were well-defined and easily enforced by the marketplace. Anything without an ISBN was not stocked by a store. The supply chain—publisher to wholesaler and/or distributor to retailer—was (and still is, for print books) complex, and the ISBN serves as a way to track and identify different versions of books.

But then digital book technology came along, and along with it, Amazon's position that an ISBN for eBooks is not required. Amazon uses something called ASIN, or Amazon Standard Identification Number, to identify eBooks sold on Amazon (Barnes & Noble has their equivalent called the BNID). Even Apple was forced to abandon its initial requirement for ISBNs lest it miss out on the rapidly expanding reader appetite for eBooks.

The ISBN requirement for eBooks is up to individual distributors or stores (i.e., the Amazon Kindle store or Apple iBooks store), and these major stores have declared it optional. Until early 2013 there was some debate about whether an identical eBook sold by numerous stores required a different ISBN for each file format. The most common example of this is a Kindle eBook, which is sold only by Amazon, versus an EPUB file which is the format sold by the other eBook retailers.

The position of the leading book trade association, the Book Industry Study Group, is that "digital books of differing file formats should be assigned different identifiers" but that "… it is not always necessary that each identifier be an ISBN."[4]

So if you opt to assign an ISBN to your eBook, this ISBN can be used for all eBook files where the content is identical. Only if the content differs do you need a separate ISBN.

Ten ISBN fundamentals

Let's begin by covering the basics. First, here are what I consider to be the six most important rules or facts to be aware of.

1. You do *not* need an ISBN to sell an eBook in the largest online stores.
2. You *do* need an ISBN to sell a print book in a store.

3. A print book and its eBook equivalent cannot share an ISBN.

4. If you change the book beyond fixing typos, you need a new ISBN.

5. There is no such thing as an eISBN.

6. You cannot reuse an ISBN.

1: You don't need an ISBN to sell eBooks in the big stores.

Based on industry research and my company's own detailed survey,[5] the overwhelming majority of eBooks sold in the United States are sold by five retailers, and these retailers do not require publishers to use an ISBN. Those retailers are Amazon, Apple, Barnes & Noble, Google, and Kobo. The other eBook retailers—and there are many—may have different rules.

2: You need an ISBN for print books intended for sale in stores.

You can't escape this requirement, but many printers and publishing services firms will provide an ISBN as part of your contract. For example, Amazon's KDP Print service is by far the largest registrant of ISBNs for independent publishers (85% in 2017), and they have two options including free and the option of using their own ISBN. (They also make it easy for publishers to buy an ISBN for a discounted price of $99.)

One important drawback when using these "free" ISBNs is that *Books In Print*, an official resource for information about books using an ISBN, will show the name of the company that assigned the ISBN for your use. This does not create any copyright or ownership problems for your book, but if you want to ensure that your *own* name is listed as the publisher, you must purchase your own ISBN (also see #9 below and the next section, **Twenty-three frequently asked questions**).

Ultimately, your decision about using an ISBN depends on how you plan to sell and distribute your book. For example, if you are selling direct to business clients or publishing a book for your family, an ISBN is unnecessary. Your distribution plans dictate whether you need an ISBN.

3: A print book and its eBook equivalent cannot share an ISBN.

An ISBN identifies a *specific version* of a book, such as print or eBook, but only one ISBN is necessary for the eBook. As noted above, these eBooks do not need different ISBNs, and in fact it is up to the stores whether they need one at all.

Follow this simple rule: if the content differs, and you are assigning an ISBN, the ISBNs must be different numbers.

Examples of book formats that can be assigned a unique ISBN include:

- Hardcover books
- Paperback books
- Spiral-bound books
- eBooks (Kindle [a.k.a. Mobi] and/or EPUB)
- Audiobooks

The reality is that the vast majority of independent publishers produce their book in just two or three of these formats, such as a paperback and an eBook in both Kindle and EPUB formats. In this example, two ISBNs are sufficient, one for the print and one for both versions of the eBook. Again, this assumes you decided to use an ISBN for your eBook. Otherwise, you need an ISBN only for the print edition.

4: If you change the book beyond fixing typos, you need a new ISBN.

Fixing errors, hyperlinks, grammar, and typos does not necessitate the assignment of a new ISBN.[6] But let's say some information presented in your book changes and you need to update it to remain accurate or relevant. You've probably seen books marketed as an "expanded and revised edition." Changes like this often make the previous edition obsolete. Using a separate ISBN distinguishes the book from the prior edition, and will in fact result in the book

receiving a new listing (in the case of online stores). This also helps used print book retailers differentiate prior print editions.

5: There is no such thing as an eISBN.

There are no special varieties of ISBNs. In fact, a game or toy can have an ISBN. As I pointed out above, there are several forms of printed books as well as several types of electronic books, not to mention audiobooks (is an ISBN for an audiobook an "aISBN"?).

6: You cannot reuse an ISBN.

This isn't one of those rules that means you "shouldn't" reuse it. Reusing a previously assigned ISBN creates confusion in the marketplace and supply chain. (Note: as described above in #3, fixing typos in an existing book is acceptable and is not considered a reuse of an ISBN.)

Once your book has been entered in the Bowker *Books In Print* database, it is automatically distributed to many other databases over which you have no control. If you reuse an ISBN, there will be two books in circulation with the same number. Which book do you want distributors and retailers to order? Also, don't forget that Amazon and other retailers use the ISBN to market used books. There is a permanent market for used print books, and an

ISBN is the only way to differentiate one edition from another.

Four more considerations

Now that we have the basics established, let's look at the final four facts to be considered.

7: Only books with an ISBN appear in industry databases.

Only books (or eBooks) with an ISBN can be listed in industry book directories. And it's these industry book directories that bookstores, libraries, and schools use to look up or order books. Depending on your marketing plans, this could be important.

8: ISBN requirements are dictated by wholesalers as well as stores.

Similar to #7, some wholesalers (such as Ingram-Spark) and stores require an ISBN, even for eBooks. So you need an ISBN if it is important for your book to be included in the broadest selection of eBook retailers.

9: ISBN ownership is unrelated to copyright.

ISBN ownership or control is unrelated to copyright ownership and control. For example, if you publish using Amazon's KDP Print and use their free ISBN option, you are not giving KDP Print any special ownership of your book. The publisher name will be listed as *Independently published*, but you can de-list it from KDP Print at any time or sell your publishing rights to the book.

10: Industry databases display the owner of the ISBN as publisher.

Even though there is no connection between ISBN ownership and copyright ownership, there are those who simply don't like the idea of another entity being listed as the publisher for their book. And this is what happens when you use an ISBN provided by another entity. Whether that's ego or pride talking, listing your name as the publisher builds credibility and your publishing brand, assuming that is one of your goals. (Also see: *My Publishing Imprint: How to Create a Self-Publishing Book Imprint & ISBN Essentials* (2019).

There is also search engine optimization (SEO) value in being listed as the publisher. (See **Appendix B**.)

For ultimate flexibility, I recommend buying ISBNs in your name as the publisher.

Protecting Book Reviews

If you are planning to publish a print book, it pays to keep in mind that reviews on Amazon (and other stores) are generally tied to your ISBN. If

you decide to make a change that requires a new ISBN, any reviews may remain with the old ISBN.

For example, let's say you used a "free" ISBN provided by Author Solutions or KDP Print and later decide you would prefer to be listed as the publisher, or that you would like to print the book elsewhere to improve your profit margin. You will need a new ISBN. Depending on the order of steps you follow to replace the old book with the new one, the reviews for your previous edition may not transfer to the new book because the ISBN is different.

Twenty-three frequently asked questions

1. How much are ISBNs?

Each country has a public or private agency that determines price. In some countries, such as Canada, they are free. Publishers based in the U.S. pay $125 for one, $295 for 10, $575 for 100, or $1500 for 1,000. However, there are a handful of resellers authorized by Bowker, notably IngramSpark and KDP Print, which sell single ISBNs that can be registered in your name for $85 and $99, respectively.

2. Where do you buy ISBNs?

R.R.Bowker, often simply referred to as Bowker, is the exclusive sales agent in the United States. With limited exceptions (as with the KDP Print example), an ISBN assigned by anyone else will not identify you as the publisher. Visit the Bowker website at MyIdentifiers.com for more information and refer to the **Resources** section at the end of this book for links to ISBN agencies for other countries.

3. Do I need an ISBN for an eBook?

Amazon Kindle, Apple iBooks, Barnes & Noble Nook, Google Play Books, and Kobo Books do not require an ISBN. Other online stores may require an ISBN and if they do, they may provide it free. Requirements also vary if you opt to use an aggregator to distribute your eBook to multiple stores. See the appendix for a table of eBook aggregators and ISBN requirements.

4. Can't I get a free (or cheap) ISBN?

Yes, sort of. Some publishing services firms will make it available for "free" while others may charge a few dollars. But keep in mind that you won't be listed as the publisher. For example, Smashwords and Amazon KDP Print both have a free ISBN option as long as you use their

company to distribute your book (and print it in the case of KDP Print). If you want to terminate your arrangement with these companies, you will need to obtain a different ISBN.

I am aware of one website that sells single ISBNs for $19 and claims you must have one to publish an eBook on Apple iBooks. This is not true.[7] Apple *previously* required an ISBN to publish an eBook in the Apple iBooks store, but not any longer. (Note that Smashwords states you need an ISBN because Apple and Kobo require them. Apple and Kobo *do not require an ISBN* if you distribute your eBook through their systems— an ISBN is a Smashwords requirement.)

5. What's the catch with a free ISBN?

Your name won't be listed as the publisher. ISBNs are *assigned* to the entity that reserved (bought) the number. If you get one free as part of a publishing arrangement, the master record will show the company that bought the ISBN, not the name of your publishing company. You are also dependent on this entity to accurately and completely enter all the details that describe your book, such as subject categories and descriptions.

If it is important for you to be listed as the publisher, you should buy your own ISBN.

6. When is an ISBN required?

It is up to the store selling your book or eBook whether you need an ISBN. In fact, if your book will never be sold in a store, you do not need an ISBN. *All major print book distributors and retailers require an ISBN.* The major eBook stores (Kindle, Nook, Kobo, and iBooks) do not require an ISBN.

7. What if I have published a book or eBook and I am changing some of its content? Do I need a new ISBN or can I use the old one?

The official position is that you need to assign a new ISBN unless you are making minor changes such as fixing typos. Adding more information or changing the contents requires a new ISBN.

8. Can you use the same ISBN for both Kindle and EPUB files?

Yes, as long as the content is the same. But you should use a separate ISBN if the content differs between eBooks. For example, if one has video and the other does not, each should have its own ISBN.

9. Do I need a new ISBN if I change the cover but keep the book's content the same?

No, this is optional. Only if you change the book's title, subtitle, dimensions, format, or interior content do you need an ISBN.

10. Do I need a new ISBN if all I want to do is reprint my book?

No, use the same ISBN.

11. What if I am publishing my book in a foreign language?

The publisher needs to assign a unique ISBN for each foreign language edition of a book.

12. Do I have to get an ISBN for every country in which I want to sell my book?

No. ISBNs are assigned based on the location of the publisher and you can use that ISBN to sell your book in any other country. A specific version of a book should have only one ISBN and it can be sold anywhere. For example, a book published in English in the U.S. can be sold in France without assigning a different ISBN. Only if the book is translated to French will it need a new ISBN—regardless of where it is sold.

13. How do I get a U.S. ISBN if I don't live in the U.S.?

You need to have a U.S. address. But why not get one in the country where you reside? It might even be free. See the **Resources** section for where to buy ISBNs based on publisher location.

14. Can I reuse the ISBN of a book I no longer publish?

No. Industry databases will continue to include the original ISBN with information about the book it was originally assigned to. An ISBN never expires, which is a primary reason for having a unique identifier in the first place.

15. What if my book is published by two different companies?

Each publisher will issue their own ISBN. For example, one publisher might have publishing rights for the United States, and a different publisher might have the rights to publish the book in the United Kingdom. An ISBN identifies a particular version of a book available from a specific publisher.

16. Do you put the ISBN in the eBook?

If you assign an ISBN to an eBook, I recommend you note the number on the copyright page. See the section **Buying and using your ISBN** for details and examples, as well as Copyright.

17. Do audiobooks need an ISBN?

The requirement for an ISBN is up to the audiobook distributor or store selling the audiobook (this is the same for all books). For example, Amazon's ACX assigns its own identifier while Findaway Voices requires an ISBN and will assign one free if you don't supply one yourself.

18. Does a DRM-protected eBook file require a separate ISBN from an eBook file that is not DRM-protected?

No. Applying DRM (digital rights management, also called copy protection) to an eBook file is simply a "wrapper" and does not change the content, so it does not require the issuance of a unique ISBN.[8]

19. Do I need new ISBNs if I want to sell sections of a published book?

Yes. For example, if you decide to sell chapters of a textbook or stories from a short story collection, you need an ISBN for each unit of content you plan to sell to the public. But if the chapter or short story is being sold as an eBook, then the requirement for an ISBN is no different from any other eBook: it is subject to the ISBN requirements of the store selling the eBook.

20. Do I still have to apply for copyright?

Applying for a copyright and assigning an ISBN to a book are unrelated. Having an ISBN does not provide copyright protection, nor is it required before filing for a copyright. (See **Copyright.**)

21. What is the difference between an ISBN-13 and ISBN-10?

ISBN-10 was replaced by ISBN-13 in 2007 when the International Organization for Standardization (ISO) decided to migrate books to the same standard numeric format used to identify other products around the world. They simply added the prefix "978" to the beginning of the ISBN-10 and recalculated the final number, called a check digit. More recently, as the supply of 978 ISBNs runs out, a new ISBN-13 prefix of 979 is being implemented. However, there is no ISBN-10 equivalent of the 979 prefix as there is with the 978 ISBN-13. See the **Resources** section for more information about how and when to convert between the two formats.

22. I got a free ISBN from a printer/publisher services firm and now I want to switch to a different printer/publisher services firm. Do I need a new ISBN?

Read your contract, but it is likely that you *do* need a new ISBN. Many service companies,

for example KDP Print, explain that you cannot continue to use the free ISBN they assign you if you decide to have your book printed by another company.

23. What do all the numbers mean?

Please refer to the Resources section for an explanation and diagrams of the five elements of an ISBN.

Different eBooks Need Different ISBNs

The major eBook retailers do not require publishers to use an ISBN. But if you do decide to assign an ISBN to an eBook, you should use it correctly.

Enhancing an eBook with multimedia content—audio, video, animation—creates a fundamentally different eBook than one that is simply text and images. As such, it should have its own unique ISBN (assuming you are assigning an ISBN). For example, if you create an eBook for the Amazon Kindle store and then use the Apple iTunes Author tool to create a version with embedded video clips, you must assign a different ISBN.

The reality is that simply adding a different ISBN to identify it as a different eBook does little to differentiate the book to the average shopper. I don't know many shoppers who would go so far as to compare ISBNs before making a purchase. But I do believe they would care about the differences in content. Shouldn't this be made clear to the shopper?

It is in the best interest of the publisher to ensure readers understand the differences between various versions of an eBook that share the same title. For example, if you are publishing an additional edition—perhaps it includes video or more images—it helps to add wording, such as Enhanced Edition, Multimedia Edition, Special Edition, or Includes Video.

Treat this as a marketing opportunity to differentiate your eBook, and if you assign an ISBN, use a different number for each edition.

KDP Print and ISBNs

An ISBN is mandatory when you publish a print book that you expect to sell via online book retailers, brick-and-mortar retailers, or distribute via wholesalers. If you don't already own an ISBN, some printers will assign a number from their own ISBN inventory. But the choices multiply to three when you use Amazon's KDP Print as your printer.

Why do I cover KDP Print in such detail? KDP Print alone (when they were called CreateSpace)

issued more than 85% of all ISBNs used by independent publishers for print books in 2017, up from 55% in 2012.[9] They offer two options as well as a discount if you want to use your own ISBN and don't already own one.

The option you choose depends on your goals, circumstances, and budget, so it pays to understand the pros and cons before you proceed. Since there are many other printers and author services firms, what you read here may or may not be relevant if you are working with one of them. If you do decide to use an ISBN provided by another company, ask whose name will appear as publisher, and find out if you can provide the information that will be entered into the ISBN record (covered in the next section).

Expanded Distribution

Expanded Distribution is a free, optional service, that allows you to submit a listing for your paperback book to U.S. distributors, principally Ingram's catalog. Booksellers and libraries in the United States order books from Ingram's catalog, as do booksellers and libraries outside the U.S. In addition, your paperback will be listed in several online stores such as Barnes & Noble (BN.com), BooksaMillion.com, and Indigo in Canada (chapters.indigo.ca).

This used to be a confusing choice when publishing using CreateSpace but Amazon narrowed the eligibility for enrollment to these two requirements:

1. Your book must use one of 15 trim sizes. Fortunately, these are industry standard dimensions and will meet the needs of most publishers. They claim that these are the sizes most retailers will support when it comes to putting books on their shelves. Whether this is true or not—after all, it is exceptionally rare for a self-published book to be stocked by stores—it's a requirement.

2. Your book can use an ISBN you bought, or one assigned by KDP Print. However, your book's ISBN must not have been submitted for distribution through another service. For example, if you are also using IngramSpark (a common strategy; see sidebar), you can't use Expanded Distribution. Obviously, this is not a problem since your book is already listed in the Ingram catalog via IngramSpark.

For more about Amazon's Expanded Distribution requirements, including a complete list of trim sizes supported, visit this page: http://breve.link/ryb50

TIP:

If you need a trim size that isn't supported by KDP Print's Expanded Distribution,
visit IngramSpark to check their sizes. They
support many more—plus a book published
through IngramSpark gets the same distribution as a book that uses Expanded Distribution.

For example, I have a client who wanted to
publish a small square book and needed it
available from IngramSpark. It was designed
as a 6.25" x 6.25" format and we added an
additional quarter inch to the sides to meet
IngramSpark's nearest trim size offering.
Then I returned to KDP Print and created
a custom trim size. That's right, you are not
limited to their stated trim sizes and can
select your own dimensions (with some
limitations).

ISBN options when using KDP Print

KDP Print offers two ISBN options.

Option 1: A KDP Print-assigned ISBN—FREE

Who doesn't like free? Keep in mind your publisher
name will look like this on Amazon's product detail
page when you select this option:

Product details

Paperback: 234 pages
Publisher: Independently published (April 11, 2019)
Language: English
ISBN-10: 1091792569
ISBN-13: 978-1091792562
Product Dimensions: 5.5 x 0.5 x 8.5 inches
Shipping Weight: 13 ounces (View shipping rates and policies)

Choose Option 1 only if you are on a budget and you don't mind being locked into using Amazon.

Pros	Cons
• Free	• KDP Print will be listed as your publisher • Restricted use (i.e., cannot use printers other than Amazon)

Option 2: Provide your own ISBN—cost varies

Committed publishers purchase a series of ISBNs. The cost ranges from as much as $125 for one to as little as $5.75 each if you buy 100, and much lower if you buy in larger quantities.

Like the alternative to Option 2 noted below, this is for those publishers who wish to maintain maximum flexibility and control over the details that

describe their book, collectively referred to as metadata.

Pros	Cons
• The name of your publishing company is listed, not KDP Print • You can use this number with another printer or distributor (i.e., if you decide to stop using KDP Print, you can keep using this number) • Maximum flexibility • Less expensive if you plan to publish more than one book	• Cost

Alternative to Option 2: A discounted ISBN—$99

This is a good option if it is important to be listed as the publisher and you don't want to spend $125 to buy a single ISBN direct from MyIdentifiers.com. In fact, this is one of the few legitimate ways you can buy an ISBN without paying MyIdentifiers the full price for a single number ($125).

Finding the link to get the discount is buried deep in the KDP Print help pages. After logging into KDP, click Help, then search for the term *ISBN* and look for the link under *Can I provide my own ISBN?* Or save yourself some time because I found the link for you. Just click here: http://breve.link/ryb51

The link will open the MyIdentifers.com website and you'll see one ISBN in a shopping cart. You will be directed to establish an account at MyIdentifiers. com before purchasing this option. Once the ISBN is purchased, you will return to MyIdentifiers.com to complete your book's ISBN assignment (see the next section).

Choose this option if you rarely publish but want to maintain control over your publishing brand.

Pros	Cons
• The name of your publishing company is listed, not KDP Print • You can use this number with another printer or distributor (i.e., if you decide to stop using KDP Print, you can keep using this number) • Maximum flexibility	• Cost

IngramSpark and ISBNs

IngramSpark, the sister print-on-demand service of Ingram's Lightning Source, which is positioned to serve larger publishers, is a serious alternative to Amazon's KDP Print. Targeted to the same market of self-publishers, it isn't as easy to use as KDP Print, nor is it free. However, it does offer a number of benefits and capabilities that Amazon's KDP Print lacks, notably:

- As noted earlier, a wider range of standard trim size options.
- The ability to print hardcover books.

- You can make your paperback or hardcover book available for pre-order.
- The ability to offer retailers wholesale pricing terms on par with large publishers.

Like KDP, you can use IngramSpark to manage distribution of both print and eBook formats. But unlike KDP, IngramSpark requires publishers to use an ISBN they own (for print and/or eBook).

The reason for this requirement is the same as it would be if you used another eBook aggregator such as Smashwords or Draft2Digital—Ingram-Spark needs some way to keep track of your book. The difference, however, is that IngramSpark does not offer a free ISBN option. Every print or eBook distributed by IngramSpark must have an ISBN supplied by the publisher.

If it's any consolation, IngramSpark charges the lowest single unit ISBN price available from a major reseller: only $85 compared to $125 if you buy direct from Bowker's MyIdentifiers website. (Amazon KDP Print charges $99.) Again, with this purchase you are listed as the publisher, and you can print or distribute your book or eBook independent of IngramSpark at any point in the future. (To be clear, buying an ISBN from IngramSpark is the same as buying it from MyIdentifiers.com. You, not IngramSpark, are the publisher of record.)

> If you do not plan to sell your print book in retail stores, IngramSpark will assign their own internal stock tracking number. This free option enables you to buy books that you might give away or sell directly to the public at events or via your website. Publishers can also use this option when producing advance reading copies for soliciting early reviews and feedback (see Barcodes for additional information on this topic). You can always buy an ISBN later if you change your mind.

KDP Print and IngramSpark for the Same Book

Some publishers find it beneficial to use KDP Print for the Amazon family of websites and Ingram-Spark to serve non-Amazon stores. This is only possible when you own and control your book's ISBN*.

There are a few strategic reasons for adding this layer of complexity to your distribution plans. The main reasons for using two different printers for the same book are that Ingram offers discounts on lower volumes of printing, has a stronger reputation for product quality, and, most importantly, provides more control over distribution options.

So why not use IngramSpark exclusively? Because it is not an uncommon complaint among publishers that their Ingram-printed books will sometimes show a delayed shipping notice in the buy box of the book page on Amazon. Even worse, customers ordering your book from Amazon (to be printed by Ingram) may receive an email stating that the book may not ship for days or weeks. Is this the fault of Ingram logistics, or is Amazon deliberately slowing deliveries to encourage more KDP Print business? Hard to say, but using both solves this potential customer service problem.

Buy new: $18.07
List Price: ~~$19.99~~
Save: $1.92 (10%)

FREE Shipping on your first order.
Details

FREE Delivery: **Select this option at checkout**

Temporarily out of stock.
Order now and we'll deliver when available. Details ⌄

*You could use a different ISBN for each printer but you cannot prevent or opt-out of the Ingram-Spark edition from being distributed to Amazon, or any other online retailer for that matter. Amazon's sales page allows a single paperback edition to be featured alongside the Kindle, hardcover, and audiobook formats.

One of my clients wanted to have a paperback color edition printed by IngramSpark and a black-and-white edition printed by KDP Print. Even though I assigned two different ISBNs, Amazon buried the more expensive color edition under a small text message that says, "See all 3 formats and editions." A shopper must click that link, then click the line, "> Paperback" to see the screenshot that follows:

	Price		New from	Used from
˅ Hide other formats and editions				
Kindle	$4.99		—	—
Paperback	$12.95	✓prime	$12.95	$6.37
Paperback, October 16, 2018	$17.00	✓prime	$17.00	$16.99

Note: This is the COLOR edition of this book.

That's a lot of clicking and the obvious reason why we don't sell many color editions. By the way, the line that reads, "★★Note: This is the COLOR edition of this book.★★" was written by me and was entered into the **Full Description** field on IngramSpark. I also added "Color ed." in the **Edition Description** field on IngramSpark.

Buying and assigning your ISBN

Assuming you decide to purchase an ISBN or a series of ISBNs, you'll want to take maximum advantage of your investment. This means making

it visible to the buying public and ensuring all the details about your book are entered into MyIdentifiers.com. That's how your book's information gets distributed to Bowker's *Books In Print* database, among many other industry databases.

Let's break the process into three steps:

1. Buy the ISBN(s).
2. Assign an ISBN to your book and place it on the copyright page.
3. Complete the registration of your book's ISBN on MyIdentifiers.com.

None of this is complicated or requires special knowledge, but it does require careful record keeping and attention to detail. You don't want to mix up or reuse numbers, because once assigned, it is difficult if not impossible to correct your mistakes. The book industry is a labyrinth of databases, and information is not necessarily synchronized or updated between the various databases once the book is released.

Publishing Imprints: What Name Should You Use?

Imprint name is simply another name for publisher and I always recommend using a name that is not your own (also called **Company Name** in the ISBN buying instructions below). This creates

some distance between you the *author*, and you the *publisher*. The usual rules for choosing and using publishing imprint names apply here as well: make sure someone else is not using the name you want to use.

Do you need to establish a legal entity such as an LLC or corporation? No, it's optional. But if you want to accept money in the name of your imprint you most likely will need to file for a "doing business as" (DBA) name and provide it to your bank.

For more information on this topic, including ten resources for researching publishing imprint names and considerations for choosing a DBA, see my book, *My Publishing Imprint*, a sister volume to this book and part of the Countdown to Book Launch series profiled at the end of this book.

Buying the ISBN

As an independent publisher, you will buy your ISBNs from MyIdentifiers.com. Having your own account is the only way to ensure you are listed as the publisher. With limited exceptions, such as buying an ISBN from an authorized re-seller, purchasing an ISBN from someone other than the MyIdentifiers website means you will not be listed as the publisher in industry databases.

1. Go to MyIdentifiers.com and register for an account as a **New Bowker Customer**. For the question **Organization Type**, independent publishers will want to select **Self-Publisher** or **Publisher** (this is a survey question and has no further relevance to your registration or account).

2. For the field Company Name, enter the name of your publishing imprint. This is the name that shows as publisher once you assign an ISBN to a book.

3. After registering, click to buy your ISBNs. For many new publishers, buying 10 for $295 is the most economical, but it ultimately depends on your publishing plans. You may also need a barcode—the block of vertical bars found on the back of books—for every ISBN assigned to a print book. You can purchase this from Bowker or any number of suppliers, but some printers provide it for free. Be sure to read the **Barcodes** chapter for more detail on this topic before you buy a barcode from MyIdentifiers.

TIP:

Members of the Independent Book Publishers Association (IBPA) receive a discount when buying ISBNs. For details, visit: https://www.ibpa-online.org/

Assigning an ISBN

After you complete the purchase, click **My Account** and select **Manage ISBNs**. You will be presented with a screen like the one below with all your unused numbers and **Assign Title** to the left of each number.

At this stage you have two choices. You can click **Assign Title** and add all of your book's information. Or, my preference, you can fill in basic information like book title and format for now and return after the book is completed (see **Return to MyIdentifiers** below).

There is nothing stopping you from completing all the required fields. In fact, if you have all the information, then completing them now would be the most efficient use of your time. But judging from my experience, you may be lacking the final details—metadata—for your book. In these cases, you will need to return anyway, so why not finish all these steps in one sitting?

By adding the title (or working title) and selecting the format (print book and/or eBook), you won't mix up the numbers between the different formats. You won't accidentally assign the ISBN to another book. I call this step *pre-assignment*.

So, assuming your book is not final, you click **Assign Title** and add the book title in the field labeled **Book Title.**

Note where it says **Form view** and that **Short** is selected. Only certain self-published books will need the extra fields of information available in the **Expanded** view. I cover this in more detail a bit further on in the section **Return to MyIdenti-fiers to complete registration of the book.** I

suggest leaving **Basic** selected for now and continuing the pre-assignment process.

Scroll down to the **Medium & Format** section and the first box is labeled **Medium.** Use the pulldown and select the format you will assign to this specific ISBN, most likely **Print** or **E-Book**. If you select **Print**, the **Format** options will reflect the various types of print formats such as **Hardback** and **Paperback**. If you select **E-Book** for the **Medium**, you will see the single option of **Electronic book text;** select this. You'll also see a field appear called **eBook File Type** and my advice is to ignore it—leave it blank. Bowker would love for you to assign an ISBN to every version of your eBook (PDF, EPUB, the Kindle Mobipocket file) but that would be expensive since it would use up ISBNs unnecessarily.

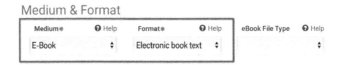

If you bought ISBNs for both print and eBook, you need to do this for each format. The next time you reach the **Medium** pull-down question, you will choose either **Print** or **E-Book**, depending on your first entry.

Now scroll down, skipping all other fields, and click **Submit**.

If you have been following my advice about pre-assigning the ISBN, you can ignore the error screen and click **OK**, or fix the errors if this is the final submission. If this is pre-assignment, the ISBN for the title you are assigning will show as incomplete until you return to complete all the required fields.

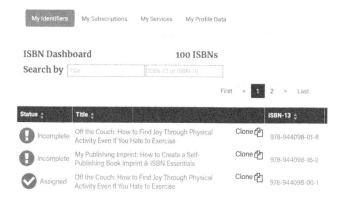

As long as you leave one of the required fields blank, you will get the error screen and be able to return to finish the assignment. Remember, the sooner you submit the final information for the assignment, the sooner your book's data will be transmitted to industry databases. However, keep in mind that not all of these databases accept revisions. This is why I recommend pre-assignment—to give you time to submit as complete a record as possible.

Same Book: One in Color, the Other Black and White

Black-and-white printing is always less expensive than color, but the unit price difference is especially great when using print-on-demand printing. Nevertheless, some publishers may want to produce editions in both formats. In these cases, you will want to assign a unique ISBN to each edition to help retailers and distributors differentiate them, and for your own record keeping purposes.

Unfortunately, the MyIdentifiers.com website does not provide a way to note this in their system. Their suggestion is to call attention to this difference in the book description field. (Also see the sidebar: KDP Print and IngramSpark for the Same Book.)

Placing the ISBN in your book

Assuming you followed my pre-assignment advice, the next step is to add the ISBN(s) to your book's copyright page (or skip ahead to finish the assignment process). You can simply copy the numbers and give them to the individual or company helping you produce your books or continue.

There is no right or wrong way to do this, but the practice I advocate is to list all the ISBNs assigned for the various formats of the book. Publishers produce books in multiple formats, and this listing serves as a form of marketing for those additional formats.

If you look at a book's copyright page—the correct location for ISBN placement—you'll likely see all sorts of implementations. One way is to show only the ISBN for the format it refers to, while omitting ISBNs for the other formats. Another is to list all the ISBNs along with the format they apply to. Sometimes the type of format precedes the ISBN in parentheses, and sometimes it comes after ... or it is not mentioned at all.

My personal preference is to list each ISBN on its own line as shown below, assuming your book is available in these formats:

- ISBN 978-0-9999999-0-9 (hardcover)
- ISBN 978-0-9999999-1-9 (paperback)
- ISBN 978-0-9999999-2-9 (eBook)

Or list them in sentence form like this:

ISBN 978-0-9999999-0-9 (hardcover), ISBN 978-0-9999999-1-9 (paperback), ISBN 978-0-9999999-2-9 (eBook)

Do you need to specify both the ISBN-13 and the old ISBN-10 number? No. The ISBN-13 standard

was implemented in 2007 and is the accepted way to identify books.

Finally, check again to make sure the ISBN you assign is for the format that you entered in MyIdentifiers. The fallback is to fix this in the next step.

TIP:

There is a need to know the ISBN–10 number if you want to create a short link to your book in the Amazon stores. This is covered in detail in the **Resources** section along with a link to a tool that converts an ISBN–13 to an ISBN–10 number, and vice versa.

Return to MyIdentifiers to complete registration of the book

As soon as you have finalized all of your book's details—the sooner the better for purposes of getting your book listed in the various databases—you need to return to MyIdentifiers to complete the book's registration. Failing to do this forfeits one of the key advantages of ownership: the book will not be listed in any of the industry databases.

Before you begin, make sure you have all the information handy. The required information is:

1. Book title (there is a subtitle field, but it is not required).

2. Contributor name and function (author name is the most obvious).
3. Medium type (print, eBook, audio).
4. Format type (depends on your choice for medium).
5. Primary subject (called "Subjects and Genres, First Genre" in your account).
6. Sales and pricing information, such as at least one country where the book will be sold, status, publication date, target audience, currency, price, and price type (as in net, wholesale, retail, etc.).

In addition to the above minimum requirements, there are four more descriptive book elements, or metadata, that Bowker uses to enhance your book listing in industry databases. It is helpful to have the following items handy or prewritten before you begin. Here is a recommended checklist:

1. Cover image in JPEG format: file size between 4KB and 5MB.
2. Book description: 350 word maximum. (They call it "Describe your book.")
3. Contributor bios (for each person): 350 word maximum.
4. Second Genre (category).

Using Advanced form view

In 2019 Bowker divided ISBN registration into two types, **Basic** and **Advanced**. **Basic** is the core metadata and you can enter your book's information using a single screen and be done with it.

The **Advanced** form view displays all the metadata fields, just the way it was done prior to the 2019 change. You need **Advanced** to enter information such as:

- Edition and volume numbers
- Copyright Year
- Library Congress Control Number (LCCN)
- Additional Medium options (for example, video or multimedia)
- Additional Format options (for example, spiral binding and board book)
- Packaging details such as how many books fit in a carton and its weight
- Additional sales information and sales information for other countries

None of this is required metadata and for many books—especially if you are publishing using POD or eBook—much of it is irrelevant. For example, you need to use **Advanced** if you want to enter your LCCN but the number of books in a carton and their weight is most useful for brick and

mortar retailers that order books from a publisher's warehouse.

Use your judgment and think in terms of someone ordering your book. If in doubt, add the information and return later if you need to change it.

Be consistent; clone titles if possible

The key is to be consistent in completing these fields for each version of the book. In other words, use the same description and cover for both the print book and the eBook ISBN records (assuming, of course, that the books are exactly the same).

That's it! Thankfully, it is a one-time effort and the good news is that you can click the **Clone** link to duplicate your entry and then edit the **Format & Size** fields for each edition. This is obviously ideal if you are completing both print and eBook registrations for the same book at the same time.

Completing your ISBN record is important for securing the benefits of owning an ISBN, so don't overlook this step.

Bulk Upload ISBN Metadata

Registering ISBNs manually is simple for self-publishers, who are defined by Bowker as creating one to ninety-nine new titles per year. But you can you

imagine how much work this would be if a publisher is publishing 500 titles per year?

The preferred solution for larger publishers to manage ISBN registration is Bowker's Excel upload form or ONIX. Both provide the ability to add and update ISBN metadata electronically instead of manually.

For more information, click the HELP > ISBN option on MyIdentifiers.com or visit the Title Submissions help page on the main Bowker website via this link: http://breve.link/ryb1

3

Barcodes

Many of you reading this book may not need to buy a barcode. I say that because many independent publishers and self-publishing authors often use print-on-demand (POD) printers like Amazon's KDP Print and IngramSpark, and these printers can produce the barcode as part of the printing process—for free.

The book cover file you submit will have a blank area on the back—this is where their printing presses place the barcode *for your specific book* at the time it is printed. Consequently, the barcode for your book does not have to be part of the cover file (see the sidebar Book Cover Templates for more information about templates for these two printers).

When you do not need a barcode

There are two instances when you do not need a barcode:

1. When your book will not be sold in a store. It is the retailer that requires the barcode, so if your book will be given away or sold outside of a store (such as through your website or at a speaking event), a barcode is not necessary. As discussed earlier, that also means an ISBN may not be necessary.

2. When producing books called advance reading copies (ARCs). Publishers print ARCs to give to prospective reviewers and other key influencers in advance of the release date. Generally speaking, ARCs are undergoing final proofing, and additional content may still be added or changed. The quality of the ARC itself may be subpar (lesser quality paper; black and white vs. color interior).

When you do need a barcode

Barcodes are required for books sold in stores. Usually these include the book's price as part of the barcode block, but it is not uncommon to leave the price off the barcode since most independently published books will not be stocked in physical stores. Also, if you order a print run to create an inventory of books and later change the price, you will need to print stickers to cover the old barcode or print new books with the new price.

On the other hand, not including the price as part of the barcode is a clear signal to book sellers and other industry professionals that your book is a print-on-demand book. Even though the largest publishers use POD, it is nonetheless closely associated with self-publishing. Including the price helps your book avoid this additional scrutiny.

If your book is being printed by KDP Print or IngramSpark, for example, and you choose not to include the price as part of the barcode, the number where the price goes will show 90000 as illustrated below. This tells a store scanner to pull the price from the store's database.

ISBN 978-0-9960739-0-5

9 780996 073905

90000

KDP Print and barcodes

Books ordered from KDP Print will have one of two types of barcodes:

1. The production or official barcode is printed on your book once you approve it for publishing.
2. The barcode on books ordered as proofs do not have the ISBN as part of the barcode. They also have a ribbon band around the cover that says "Not for Resale." By the way, this barcode is larger than the official barcode printed on final books so it might cover text in this area on proof copies. That won't be the case for the final version of your book if you followed the instructions for the template. The Not for Resale ribbon band and this barcode are new changes implemented during the conversion from CreateSpace to KDP Print. See example below.

During the upload procedure you can tell KDP Print that you are including the barcode as part of your cover. If your template does not include a barcode, the KDP Print-printed barcode will show 90000 where the price normally goes. Unlike IngramSpark, you do not have the option of adding a price to this automatically created barcode.

To include the price in the barcode, you must upload a cover that includes a barcode. If you plan to offer your book in physical stores, you might be safer following the directions below to include a barcode with the price as part of your cover file when you upload it to KDP Print. If this is the case, it is a simple and inexpensive purchase. You can do

this yourself, or your book designer can handle it for you.

For quick reference, here are the KDP Print barcode requirements as of 2019. Note that its location cannot be changed (bottom right; see the Book Cover Templates sidebar later in this chapter).

- 2" (50.8 mm) wide and 1.2" (30.5 mm) tall
- At least .25" (6 mm) from the cover's edge
- Image quality:
  » Vector images are preferred
  » At least 300 dots per inch if the barcode is rasterized
  » Solid white background
  » Barcode is 100% black (not colors or registration black)
- Right-side up and square to the cover
- Not flattened into main cover as one single image

You can include a QR Code or UPC barcode in addition to the ISBN barcode, but it can't appear in the space reserved for the ISBN barcode.

IngramSpark and barcodes

There are three barcode options when using IngramSpark.

1. A barcode that represents an IngramSpark-assigned number for books without an ISBN. For example, you may not want to assign an ISBN to books printed as advance reading copies (ARCs). This will help prevent the ARCs from being resold in stores and online, which require books to have an ISBN. Once you print the ARCs and finalize your book, you must contact IngramSpark and ask them to change your book's serial number to the ISBN you plan to assign to the book.

2. A barcode with the book's price. Unlike KDP Print, IngramSpark will produce the barcode with your book's price as part of the printing process.

3. A barcode without a price. Like KDP Print, the barcode will show 90000 where the price normally goes.

How to produce a barcode

There are scores of resources for obtaining barcodes in the event your designer or printer does not provide one for you. A convenient option is the company that sells you your ISBNs: Bowker, via MyIdentifiers.com. Their standard charge $25 each, but they often run sales where they include one free when you buy 10 ISBNs.

David Wogahn

A source I've used for years is AaronGraphics. Their price is $15, and for that they email you (or your designer) a Mac or Windows EPS file that matches your ISBN and price. Another experienced provider of barcode files is Barcode Graphics (self-service is $10).

Both AaronGraphics (http://breve.link/ryb2) and Barcode Graphics (http://breve.link/ryb3) are experts at creating barcodes as files or printing them on stickers for any kind of product. As I mentioned earlier, if you include your book's price as part of the barcode, and later change the price, you need to cover the old price on any printed books you have, assuming you plan to sell them in stores. These companies can create the labels you need to cover the old barcode.

TIP:

I cannot recommend buying a barcode from MyIdentifiers.com. They make it seem necessary when you buy your ISBNs but their barcode is overpriced and you might not need it. And are you certain about your book's price when you place that order? In my experience, you are not. Wait and see.

Where to place the barcode

A common location is on the back bottom right corner—and in fact this is a KDP Print requirement. IngramSpark templates show the location at middle-bottom, but state that it can be moved to any location on the back cover template. However, this is generally influenced, if not dictated, by the cover template you use. The template itself will show a blank space where the barcode will be printed when the book is produced. Discuss this with your cover designer and/or your printer.

Book Cover Templates

I suspect many readers of Register Your Book will use either KDP Print or IngramSpark to print their book. Both have an online tool you can use to produce a cover template specific for your book. You input options—like dimensions (trim size), number of pages, paper type, etc.—and receive one or more files that you provide to your designer or use yourself.

• The KDP Print cover template generator and instructions are found at http://breve.link/ryb4. This template does not include the barcode. You will need to add it or use the free barcode printed by KDP Print.

- IngramSpark's Cover Template Generator can be found at http://breve.link/ryb5. This template does include the barcode.

Finding the price in a barcode

The large block of vertical bars describes the ISBN in machine-readable terms. The smaller block to the right is for the price. When you print the price, it will be preceded by a 5, used to indicate that the price is denominated in U.S. dollars. In the example below, the price is $49.95.

4

Copyright

Assuming you have the right to file a copyright on your book, this chapter explains how to do it, why you would want to do so as soon as possible, and the consequences if you don't. This chapter also goes into detail about the required and optional contents for a copyright page.

The United States Copyright Office implemented new processing and pricing in May 2014. A key element of this change was to make the cost and process for registering an author's copyright as easy and inexpensive as possible. If you are the sole author of a single work that is not made-for-hire, the process is simple and costs $35. Otherwise, the standard filing fee is $55. Both assume the registration is filed online; paper filings are $85. (http://breve.link/ryb6)

The author who includes material that is copyrighted by others should consult with a lawyer familiar with copyright. Things like extensive quotes, song lyrics, and photographs may need to be cleared with the owners of those copyrights. At a minimum you need to acknowledge their rights, and an attorney can clarify this for you.

The following information is provided as a general guide and not as a substitute for legal advice or counsel.

Why filing for a copyright is important

The important things to know about copyright are why it is necessary and how to secure it. Technically your book is "protected" as soon as it is in a "fixed medium of expression" or otherwise published, but initiating legal action is easier if your book has been registered. Timing is also important. Here is a summary of four key points found in *Circular 1, Copyright Basics* from Copyright.gov:

- Registration is necessary for works of U.S. origin *before* an infringement suit may be filed in court. In fact, a 2019 U.S. Supreme Court ruling (Fourth Estate v. Wall-Street.com) affirmed that a copyright registration must have been granted by the Copyright Office, not simply filed, before copyright litigation may commence. As noted in the previous edition of this book, copyright rules are often subject to court/judicial interpretation.

» If registration is made within three months after publication of the work or prior to an infringement of the work, statutory damages and attorney's fees will be available to the copyright owner in court actions. Otherwise, only an award of actual damages and profits is available to the copyright owner.

» Registration allows the owner of the copyright to record the registration with the U.S. Customs Service for protection against the importation of infringing copies. (For additional information, visit the U.S. Customs and Border Protection website at cbp.gov.)

» If made before or within five years of publication, registration will establish *prima facie* evidence in court of the validity of the copyright and of the facts stated in the certificate. (Simply put, if you assert your right to copyright, the other party will need to prove you wrong—a far better position for you because this is easier than you having to prove you are right.)

As of June 2019, it takes one to seven months (a four-month average) to process electronic applications and one to eighteen months (a seven-month average) to process applications submitted by mail. The processing time varies—these are estimates. (In the 2016 edition of this book it took an average of eight months to process applications submitted online and an average of 13 months for applications submitted by mail.) Regardless of the processing time, the effective date of registration is the date the Copyright Office received the completed application, correct payment, and copy(ies) of the work being registered in acceptable form. You do not need to wait for a certificate to proceed with publication.

If you were to wait and register after discovering an infringement, the minimum cost to expedite processing (necessary if you are taking legal action; see the first bullet in the preceding list) is $800, and other fees may apply. This cost is subject to change. (For comparison purposes, it was $550 as recently as 2016.)

A second compelling reason to register immediately is that you can collect statutory damages and attorney's fees if there is a court action. While your case may never get to this point, the fact that you

can collect these damages and fees is a powerful deterrent to infringing parties.

By the way, there is no provision in copyright law supporting what is sometimes called "the poor man's copyright"—the practice of mailing yourself a copy of your book. This is not a substitute for registration.

For answers to frequently asked questions about copyright, please visit http://breve.link/ryb7.

Preparing to register a copyright

The cost to register a copyright electronically begins at $35. This is for a *Single Application,* which is defined as a single author submitting a single work on their own behalf with no other authors or rights holders involved. You fill out the form online and include your book in one of these formats:

- .doc (Microsoft Word Document 2003 or earlier)
  - » .docx (Microsoft Word Open XML Document)
  - » .htm, .html (HyperText Markup Language)
  - » .pdf (Portable Document Format)
  - » .rtf (Rich Text Format)
  - » .txt (Text File)

» .wps (Microsoft Works Word Processor Document)

» .fdr (Final Draft)

(For a complete list of acceptable formats, please visit http://breve.link/ryb8. Maximum upload file size is 500MB. In the unlikely event that your book exceeds this size, you will have to follow the instructions for submitting files via mail.)

You also have the option of adding additional contacts, such as an attorney, or you can list your name as the sole contact for each role. Here are the roles from Copyright.gov in case you want to prepare this ahead of time:

- **Claimants**: The copyright claimant(s) in this work. The author is the original copyright claimant. The claimant may also be a person or organization to whom copyright has been transferred.

  » **Rights & Permissions**: Contact information for a person and/or organization to be contacted regarding copyright management information or permission to use this work. If you prefer not to provide personally identifying information, you may list a third-party agent or a post office box.

» **Correspondent**: The person the Copyright Office will contact if it has questions about this application. Completion of the name, email address, and correspondence address is mandatory.

» **Mail Certificate**: The name and address to which the registration certificate should be mailed. Completion of Individual and/ or Organization Information, and Address is mandatory.

Once you have gathered your files and the contact information you plan to use, visit the Copyright. gov website at http://breve.link/ryb9 and register for an account. You can also access tutorials and check current processing time. By the way, you can pause the process at any time and return to complete your application.

Log in to the Electronic Copyright Office (eCO) Registration System

Registration Processing Times and FAQs

Literary Works
Fiction, Non-Fiction, Poetry, Articles, Periodicals

Performing Arts
Music, Lyrics, Sound Recordings, Scripts, Stage Plays

Should You Preregister a Copyright on Your Book?

The copyright office discourages preregistration of copyrights and, in fact, backs that up with a few disincentives such as a $140 filing fee. This is in addition to the formal registration process and fee, which must still be completed once the book is finalized. It bears emphasizing that preregistration is not registration.

Copyright preregistration is only really necessary for subject matter or authors who have had a history of prerelease infringement. This does not typically apply to the average independent publisher or self-published author, but it's been a problem in the past for copyright holders of film and music compositions as well as authors working through

an agent to shop a book proposal to traditional publishers. Learn more here: http://breve.link/ryb10.

How to format your copyright page

The copyright page is part of what is called the "front matter" of your book and it is one of the few mandatory pages of any book. The appropriate location is the back of the title page, which means it is a left-facing ("verso") page.

It's also specific to the contents of the book in which it is placed (sort of like a food label). There may be past editions or different formats of the book, but *this* copyright page is specific to *this* specific version or edition of the book. So, for example, while "Printed in the U.S.A." can be entirely appropriate on the printed book's copyright page, it is irrelevant and should not be part of an eBook's copyright page.

I have divided the information that can appear on this page into three groups: mandatory, typical, and additional (if applicable).

Mandatory copyright page content

This is your copyright notice. Yes, this is the only required information for this page. In the words of the U.S. Copyright Office, the following must be included:

1. The symbol © (the letter C in a circle), or the word "Copyright," or the abbreviation "Copr."
2. The year of first publication of the work
3. The name of the owner of copyright in the work, an abbreviation by which the name can be recognized, or a generally known alternative designation of the owner

Example: © 2019 David Wogahn

(This notice would look slightly different if you incorporate someone else's copyrighted information, or if your book incorporates U.S. government works, which are not eligible for copyright protection. In these cases, you should contact an attorney or refer to the publication Copyright Basics available from the U.S. Copyright Office: http://breve.link/ryb11.)

Do you need to include "All Rights Reserved"?

The short answer: no, but it removes any ambiguity as to rights when you do add it. In other words, it doesn't hurt to add it.

Each country specifies the appropriate language to use when declaring copyright and defers to international treaties and agreements to inform those requirements. Until August 23, 2000, the United States was a party to an agreement (Buenos Aires Convention, 1910) which required all 17 national

signatories to use the phrase *All Rights Reserved.*[10] U.S. copyright law now conforms to the Berne Convention, which makes copyright automatic (as noted above).

Typical copyright page content

1. The copyright notice as discussed above
2. Legal notices (included in the next section are 13 sample notices)
3. ISBN information. As discussed in the chapter on ISBNs, I recommend listing all numbers assigned to the various formats of your book (e.g., print, eBook, audiobook).
4. Contact information for the publisher

This last piece of information—publisher contact information—is something I see many indie publishers struggle with. Should it be your name? The name of your imprint or publishing company? How much contact information should you provide? After all, including it is optional.

The information to include is entirely up to you and depends on your objectives. Chances are, you have an *About the Author* section in the back of your book, along with contact information such as your website or email address. So the information you place here is how you wish to be contacted if someone has a question about the book. For example,

someone may wish to sell it in their store, purchase copies directly from the publisher ... or maybe even offer you a licensing or publishing arrangement.

Another objective for many independent publishers is to distance themselves from their dual role of author and publisher. Many media and public relations professionals still have an aversion to promoting self-published books (not to mention that some readers feel the same way, although this is changing).

For purposes here, I suggest that you (at a minimum) include an email that is not your name. If you have a name for your publishing company, list it along with whatever contact information you wish to share.

For more information about publishing imprints, including why and how to set one up, please see *My Publishing Imprint: How to Create a Self-Publishing Book Imprint & ISBN Essentials* (David Wogahn, 2019).

Additional copyright page content

These remaining elements may or may not apply to you. But if they do, be sure to include them.

1. Library of Congress information. If you secured this information, you must include it on the

copyright page. This is covered in detail in a following chapter.

2. If this is not the first edition of the book, you will want to include the edition number.

3. Printer's Key. You may have noticed that some books have rows of numbers like this:

10 9 8 7 6 5 4 3 2 1

Or with two-digit years included, like this:

22 21 20 19 18 17 16   1 2 3 4 5 6 7 8 9 10

This practice originated in the early days of using physical plates to print books and is still in use by publishers to keep track of print runs, and sometimes the years in which they occur. As new print runs are ordered, the lowest number is removed and the two-digit year, when present, represents the year that printing took place. If you were using printing plates, the printer could simply scratch off a number rather than produce new plates. Digital printing and POD have rendered this practice irrelevant. However, some POD publishers use the Printer's Key to keep track of minor edition changes. You can learn more here: http://breve.link/ryb12.

4. Contributors. Like other creative projects, a book is often the result of the production efforts of several contributors, such as an editor, proofreader,

designer, and/or indexer. A publisher is not necessarily required to list their names and roles, but it is not uncommon to acknowledge those who made a significant creative contribution to the book. This is entirely up to the publisher.

(This should not be confused with an acknowledgments page, which is where the author has a chance to acknowledge and thank people. The copyright page is for the publisher's use—an important distinction if you are performing both roles.)

5. Environmental notices. Some publishers make a point of using recycled paper or following environmentally friendly best practices. Check with your printer to see what types of paper and printing practices they follow and whether you might include wording or relevant logos in this regard. For more information on this topic visit the Forest Stewardship Council (https://us.fsc.org/en-us) and the Environmental Paper Network (https://environmentalpaper.org/) websites for more information.

Bottom line: this is your official business page. Review the copyright page of this book and the copyright page of other professionally produced books to see all these elements at work.

Sample copyright legal notices

The use of copyright notices and disclaimers on the copyright page is entirely up to you, the publisher. They can be non-existent, brief, or quite detailed—something you need to decide in consultation with your legal advisor.

I am not an attorney, nor am I providing legal advice, but anyone can pick up a book and copy the notices and disclaimers used by another publisher.

Each of these thirteen examples is from a book with content intended for a specific audience. Be sure to contact an attorney about your specific needs and circumstances, then add your legal notice to your copyright page.

Example 1: General

Without limiting the rights under copyright reserved above, no part of this publication may be reproduced, stored in or introduced into a retrieval system, or transmitted in any form or by any means (electronic, mechanical, photocopying, recording, or otherwise), without the prior written permission of both the copyright owner and the above publisher of this book, except by a reviewer who wishes to quote brief passages in connection with a review written for insertion in a magazine, newspaper, broadcast, website, blog, or other outlet.

Example 2: General

This book is intended to provide accurate information with regards to its subject matter. However, in times of rapid change, ensuring all information provided is entirely accurate and up-to-date at all times is not always possible. Therefore, the author and publisher accept no responsibility for inaccuracies or omissions and specifically disclaim any liability, loss or risk, personal, professional or otherwise, which may be incurred as a consequence, directly or indirectly, of the use and/or application of any of the contents of this book.

Example 3: General

The publisher does not have any control over and does not assume any responsibility for author or third-party websites or their content. The scanning, uploading, and distribution of this book via the Internet or via any other means without the permission of the publisher is illegal and punishable by law. Please purchase only authorized electronic editions, and do not participate in or encourage electronic piracy of copyrighted materials. Your support of the author's rights is appreciated.

Example 4: General

While the author has made every effort to provide accurate telephone numbers and Internet addresses at the time of publication, neither the publisher nor the author assumes any responsibility for errors or for changes that occur after publication. Further, the publisher does not have any control over and does not assume any responsibility for author or third-party websites or their content.

Example 5: General

All other trademarks are the property of their respective owners. Screenshots are used for illustrative purposes only.

Example 6: Books that Reference Trademarks

Many of the designations used by manufacturers and sellers to distinguish their products are claimed as trademarks. Where those designations appear in this book and the publisher was aware of a trademark claim, the designations have been printed in caps or initial caps.

Example 7: Legal, Financial, General

Although the publisher and author have used reasonable care in preparing this book, the information it contains is distributed "as is" and without warranties of any kind. This book is not intended as legal or financial advice, and not all of the recommendations may be suitable for your situation. Professional legal and financial advisors should be consulted as needed. Neither the publisher nor the

author shall be liable for any costs, expenses, or damages resulting from use of or reliance on the information contained in this book.

Example 8: Legal, Medical, Professional

This book is written and published to provide accurate and authoritative information relevant to the subject matter presented. It is published and sold with the understanding that the author and publisher are not engaged in rendering legal, medical, or other professional services by reason of their authorship or publication of this work. If medical, legal, or other expert assistance is required, the services of a competent professional person should be sought.

Example 9: Fiction

This is a work of fiction. The events and characters described herein are fictitious and otherwise imaginary and are not intended to refer to specific places or living persons. The opinions expressed in this book are solely the opinions of the author and do not represent the opinions or thoughts of the publisher. The author has represented and warranted full ownership and/or legal right to publish all the materials contained in this book.

Example 10: Fiction

This is a work of fiction. The events and persons are imagined. Any resemblance to actual events, or to persons, alive or dead, is purely coincidental.

Example 11: Fiction

This is a work of the imagination in its entirety. All names, settings, incidents, and dialogue have been invented, and when real places, products, and public figures are mentioned in the story, they are used fictionally and without any claim of endorsement or affiliation. Any resemblance between the characters in the novel and real people is strictly a coincidence.

Example 12: Medical and Health

The author of this book does not dispense medical advice or prescribe the use of any technique as a form of treatment for physical or medical problems without the advice of a physician, either directly or indirectly. The intent of the author is only to offer information of a general nature to help you in your quest for emotional and spiritual well-being. In the event you use any of the information in this book for yourself, which is your constitutional right, the author and the publisher assume no responsibility for your actions.

Example 13: Medical and Health

This book is intended to supplement, not replace, the advice of a trained health professional. If you know or suspect that you have a health problem, you should consult a health professional. The author and publisher specifically disclaim any liability, loss, or risk, personal or otherwise, that is incurred as a consequence, directly or indirectly, of the use and application of any of the contents of this book.

5

Library of Congress

W ho wouldn't want their book to be part of the Library of Congress collections? Better yet, I think it's safe to say that it is the dream of every independent publisher to place a copy of their book in every library in America. Before continuing, it is important to note that:

1. You must plan ahead because it may take several weeks to complete the process (although it is often less).
2. Your book must not yet be published.
3. Your book must be available in print format.
4. There is no relationship between a copyright filing and the two Library of Congress cataloging programs discussed below.
5. You must be a U.S.-based publisher.

Understanding the two programs: CIP and PCN

The world's largest library has two programs, and they are mutually exclusive—you do not participate in both.

Cataloging in Publication (CIP) program

A Cataloging in Publication (CIP) data record is prepared by the Library of Congress (LoC) for a book in advance of its publication. The purpose of the program is to inform U.S. libraries of the *future* availability of a book, a book *most likely to be widely acquired by U.S. libraries*. When the book is finally published, the publisher includes the CIP data on the copyright page.

Publishers whose books are part of this program do not incur an additional expense to produce a cataloging block (sometimes called a data block and described further under Optional cataloging block below). More importantly, books in this program enjoy greater visibility to libraries which can translate to more sales.

However, self-published books and new publishers are excluded from participation; at least until they can meet these key eligibility requirements:

1. A publisher must have already published at least three titles, by three different authors. All three

titles must have been acquired by at least 1,000 U.S. libraries, either in print or eBook format.★

2. No print-on-demand books are accepted. This means no books printed by Amazon's KDP Print, or Ingram's Lightning Source or IngramSpark, to name three popular POD printing options.

3. No books paid for or subsidized by individual authors are accepted.

4. No eBook-only titles are accepted. (Titles published simultaneously in print and eBook are eligible.)

5. Fee-for-service publishers, book distributors, book printers, and other intermediaries are ineligible.★

★These two eligibility requirements have been clarified and updated since I first published this book in 2016:

• Regarding number one, the Library used to simply specify that the three books must be "widely acquired" by libraries. I suspect many applicants figured the Library would not or could not verify this, so they added the 1,000 library requirement and a warning label of sorts: "CIP Program staff search in WorldCat to determine how many libraries hold a copy of the titles." See the sidebar at the end of this chapter for information about WorldCat.

- Regarding number five, the company (or individual) that owns their ISBN is the publisher. They might hire someone or another firm to perform the various publishing steps (book design, eBook programming, and so on), but they are still the publisher. What the Library is referring to are vanity presses and other book intermediaries that use *their* ISBN to publish a book on behalf of the author. This is why it is so important to own your ISBN. And if you hire someone or a firm to help you, and they represent that your book will be part of the CIP program, you are most likely being duped.

Note that the list of five eligibility criteria above are highlights. If you think your publishing company qualifies, you should visit the CIP page for complete details: http://breve.link/ryb13.

Preassigned Control Number (PCN) program

Unlike the CIP program, any U.S.-based publisher or self-publisher *can* participate in the Library's Preassigned Control Number (PCN) program. Once you have a free PCN account, you then apply for a Library of Congress Control Number (LCCN). The process is simple if you plan ahead and you meet the eligibility requirements.

There is no reason why you should not apply for an LCCN, but keep in mind that a number is no guarantee of acceptance into the LoC collections. Here is their disclaimer:

> Final determination of works selected and cataloged is made by selection librarians and recommending officers in compliance with Library of Congress collection development policies upon receipt of the printed book. Please note that while a title may receive a pre-assigned control number, the Library of Congress is under no obligation to provide preliminary or final cataloging information within its catalog for titles that are not ultimately selected for the Library's permanent collection.

What books are ineligible? Books already published, eBooks, mass market paperbacks, and several other categories of materials. Here is a brief summary of the eligibility requirements:

- You must be a U.S.-based book publisher.
- You must list a place of publication on the title page or copyright page of your book(s) and maintain an editorial office in the U.S. capable of answering substantive bibliographic questions.
- The book must not yet be published.
- The book must be available in print.

Note that if you first released your book as an eBook and subsequently decide to publish it in print, your book is still considered to be published. You are simply releasing your book in an additional format.

Visit the PCN page for more details and criteria: http://breve.link/ryb14.

There are also several types of books that are excluded from the program: textbooks below the college level, religious or expendable instruction materials (such as fill-in-the-blank workbooks), serials (such as newspapers and magazines), mass market paperbacks, and translations except Spanish. For a complete list, visit: http://breve.link/ryb15.

Is it worth the effort and potential expense?

Applying for and using an LCCN does not by itself guarantee sales. But it could position your book for success should you wish to market to libraries, and the only time you can request one is before the book is published. It also lends an air of legit-imacy to your book by more closely aligning the information on the copyright page with that which traditional publishers include. This is especially true if you invest in what's called a P-CIP cataloging block.

The P-CIP cataloging block tells the librarian where to place the book in the library: "P," as in Publisher-provided Cataloging in Publication. (Publishers participating in the CIP program receive a CIP, as in Cataloging in Publication cataloging block, prepared by Library of Congress staff at no charge.)

If this information is not on the copyright page, the interested librarian has two choices: ignore the book or create the cataloging block themselves. I don't know how many books miss out on being adopted by libraries because the P-CIP information is not present, but I imagine it would be a deterrent for some librarians due to the extra work to create one. By the way, fiction books have it a little easier because those books are filed by author's last name. Considering this, a P-CIP for a self-published fiction book may not be worth the investment.

Marketing to Libraries

Deciding whether to invest time and money into the LCCN/P-CIP process depends on the likelihood of your book being acquired by libraries. Selling to libraries is like any other sales and marketing opportunity in book publishing. Independently published books that tend to be attractive to libraries fit in the category often referred to as evergreen, meaning they remain relevant for years to come. This would include history books, how-to books, reference books, directories, and books that have special local or regional appeal.

At the same time, it is entirely possible for libraries to order books directly from a self-publisher. My colleague Jeniffer Thompson from Monkey C Media shared with me that one of her authors regularly receives orders from libraries for his self-published fiction books. These are direct orders, meaning they do not come from wholesalers such as Ingram and Baker & Taylor.

My final cautionary advice is to consider how you plan to market your book to libraries. Will you attend the American Library Association tradeshow or hire a distributor to contact libraries? Will you buy advertising that markets your book to librarians?

Choose from one of two PCN account types

If you are still undecided or concerned about the work to apply for a LCCN, know that the procedure for applying for an LCCN got a whole lot easier in May 2019 when the Library launched a streamlined and modern system for creating PCN accounts and processing LCCN applications.

The old system required a two-step process for all applicants that took between hours and days to complete. Once the PCN application was approved, you had to navigate what seemed like webpages designed in 1999. No more, at least for self-publishers. The new website and process is attractive, responsive, and most importantly, self-publishers can complete the application process in a single session.

Note: If you established a PCN account prior to May 2019, you need to create a new account before submitting LCCN requests. Old accounts were not migrated to the new system.

Your choice between the two comes down to two considerations since both are viable if you own your ISBNs.

- Authors/Self-Publishers can complete the process in a single session consisting of PCN account registration and applying for an LCCN (step-by-step instructions are noted below).
- Publishers (the LoC also refers to this choice as Traditional Publishers) must follow a two-step procedure. Apply for a PCN account, wait for LoC approval, then begin submitting LCCN requests. This option is intended for use by publishers—publishing businesses that are, or are intending to, publish books by more than

one author. The primary advantage appears to be that you can appoint another individual, perhaps outside your organization, to manage the account for you.

For both programs you must apply for an LCCN in a month prior to the month you intend to release your book. For example, if this is June 1 and you plan to release your book in June, the system will not accept your request for an LCCN.

Option 1: Author/Self-Publishers step-by-step PCN and LCCN application

Visit this link and click the Create account button: http://breve.link/ryb52.

Creating your account

Enter your name, email, and a 16-character password to establish your account.

Optional: After establishing your account you can click the dot with your initials in the top right corner and select Profile to add your photo and additional contact details such as an address and additional phone numbers, or change your password.

After creating your account, click **Request LCCN**.

Assemble this checklist of items ahead of time because there is no way to save your work and return to it later. You'll have to start over.

1. Your book information, or metadata, such as title, subtitle, page count, publisher name, ISBN(s).
2. Year of birth for each contributor.
3. Publication month and year.
4. Although it is not a requirement, you have the option of submitting a PDF of the title page of your book.

Screen one: General Information

Information entered here is checked against the rules of the program. Specifically, the General Information screen asks:

- *Will the forthcoming book be published in electronic format only?* If you click Yes, you cannot get an LCCN. An LCCN is for books in print (or eBooks with a print equivalent).
- *Will the book appear at periodic intervals?* Selecting Yes will give you a message that books that appear weekly, monthly, annually, or quarterly are not eligible for an LCCN.

- *Will the book be intended for children or young adults?* A selection of Yes shows another screen asking for Grade Level and Age.
- *Approximate number of pages.* Items under 50 pages, with the exception of genealogies, children's literature, and catalog exhibitions, are not eligible for an LCCN.
- *Projected publication date.* If you use a date in the past, you receive an error message suggesting you donate your book to the Library of Congress because you cannot get an LCCN.

Once all the fields are filled-in, click Next Section.

Screen two: Contributor Information

The contributor information for most people requesting an LCCN will be as an individual. Individual is automatically selected but change it to Organization if a company name is to be used as the author.

After clicking Individual or Organization, enter your name (or organization) as it appears on the title page of your book, select Contributor Type, and click Add Contributor.

As noted in the help text, a Date of Birth is requested, but not required (year only). This assists the Library in distinguishing between similar names and omitting it may delay processing.

Add additional contributors if relevant—author, editor, illustrator, translator, complier, and other are the options.

> **TIP:** The additional contributor names added in this step are typically the same as those people you credit when submitting your book for distribution through a publishing portal such as KDP, IngramSpark, and so on. These are individuals whose contributions were fundamentally necessary and even required to complete the book. A children's book illustrator is an example of someone to include here. Your copyeditor is an example of someone you would not list here.

Click **Add Contributor** for each contributor then click Next Section when done.

Screen three: Title Page

Here is where you enter the specific details about your book such as title, subtitle, edition, publisher, and contributors—all of which must match exactly the title page of your book. In fact, if you have a title page in PDF format you can upload it. It's an optional step but doing so may speed the processing of your LCCN application.

There are two important fields to note:

1. If you have purchased ISBNs in the name of your publishing imprint, ignore the instructions under Publisher Name which state: *If you are a self-publisher, please enter your name in the field below.* Enter the publishing imprint name you used when buying your ISBN(s). Again, this same name should also be printed at the bottom of your book's title page along with the city and state where the publisher is located.

2. If you entered a contributor name in screen two that is different from the title page (for example, you entered Jen Doe on screen two and the title page says Jennifer Doe), you can edit the text box here on screen three so it matches your book's title page.

Screen four: Series & Volume Info

For most books, this page will require only a few clicks.

Series Information, Yes or No. Enter the Series Title and its Series Volume if it is part of a series. There is a field for the ISSN—International Standard Serial Number—if you have one. But in our world of book publishing this isn't relevant because ISSNs are used with newspapers, journals, magazines, and periodicals—not a series of novels or how-to books. Learn more about ISSNs here: http://breve.link/ryb53.

Volume Information, Yes or No. Selecting No, the screen asks for the ISBN for the print edition of your book and its Format (hardcover, paperback, spiral bound, and seven other options). These options are similar to the print options available when registering your ISBN using MyIdentifiers.com.

If your book consists of more than one physical volume (you answered Yes), the screen expands to ask the volume number (Vol #) and Volume Title for each volume.

The second part of the **Volume Information** section requires you to answer: *Will the book also be published in electronic format?* If you click No, click Next Section.

If you select **Yes,** you must enter an ISBN for the eBook. There are nine eBook **Format** types available to be assigned to an ISBN in this section: Adobe PDF, ebook, ebook other, EBK, epub, Kindle Edition, Mobi, Nook Edition, Other. Make sure you assign the **Format** type for your ISBN that matches what you used at MyIdentifiers.com.

Following my advice from the ISBN chapter, I recommend assigning a single ISBN to an eBook. In this case, choose the ebook format for the Format field. But if you assigned an ISBN for the Kindle Edition, choose that option. If you assigned an addition ISBN to the epub (in addition to the ISBN for the Kindle), add that ISBN as well.

If you are not assigning an ISBN to your eBook you have no choice but to answer **No** to the question: *Will the book also be published in electronic format?*

If you are using a free ISBN provided by an aggregator, do not enter that here. This field is for an ISBN that shows you as the publisher and an ISBN from an aggregator will show that aggregator as the publisher.

Screen five: Additional Info & Summary

There are two optional fields on this screen. One is space for a Book Summary; enter a description or summary of your book. It must be in English and less than 5,000 characters in length.

The second field is called **Additional Info**. The instructions say *Please use this space to communicate any information you think may be useful in the cataloging process.* This might be if your book has an index, or includes visuals such as photos or illustrations, for example.

However, as of this writing, it is unclear how information like this is used or if it helps a book in some way. If you have such information, note it here, but don't be concerned if you leave it blank. As noted earlier, this is a new system and more clarity may be added in the future.

Screen six: Confirm & Submit

Review the summary of everything you entered and click **Submit** if it is correct. Or return and make corrections.

Option 2: Publisher step-by-step PCN and LCCN application

This account type and the process of requesting an LCCN is similar to Option 1, the Author/Self-Publishers step-by-step section noted above. The primary differences are:

1. This is a two-step process. First you apply for an account. Once approved (it takes several days), you can request an LCCN. Consequently, the only time I recommend this option is if there is a chance you may publish books written by other authors.

2. Speaking of other authors, there is a button in this account type that makes it easy for publisher to apply for the CIP status noted above.

3. You can add an additional contact to your account, and they can submit applications on behalf of the publisher.

Visit this link and click the **Create account** button: http://breve.link/ryb54.

Creating your account

To create a publisher account, you will need the publisher's name and address, and contact information for those to be listed in the account. This can be the same person, or you can name two different people.

- The emails you enter are checked to see if that email is already being used for another account. If it is, you can't add it.

There are five screens to complete:

1. **Your information:** Publisher name and your contact information

2. **Publisher information:** Your publisher's U.S. address

3. Are you your **publisher's primary contact?** Yes or No. If No, add that person.

4. **Publisher senior officer:** The senior officer is responsible for the organization's compliance with PCN and CIP program policies. And they ask: *Is the publisher's senior officer the same as the primary contact?* Yes or No. If No, add the person that is.

5. The fifth screen is to **Confirm and Submit** the information you've entered. Check it thoroughly and click Submit.

It takes several days for them to review your application. If approved, you will receive an email with instructions for finishing the account setup and choosing a 16-character password.

Optional: After establishing your account you can click the dot with your initials in the top right corner and select **Profile** to add your photo and additional contact details such as an address and additional phone numbers, or change your password.

After creating your account, you will see two options: **Apply to CIP** and **Request LCCN.** As noted above, the **Apply to CIP** button is only relevant if you have already published books that meet the Cataloging in Publication (CIP) Program criteria. Since it is highly unlikely that you qualify at this stage, click **Request LCCN.**

Assemble this checklist of items ahead of time because there is no way to save your work and return to it later. You'll have to start over.

1. Your book information, or metadata, such as title, subtitle, page count, publisher name, ISBN(s).
2. Year of birth for each contributor.
3. Publication month and year.
4. Although it is not a requirement, you have the option of submitting a PDF of the title page of your book.

Screen one: General Information

Information entered here is checked against the rules of the program. Specifically, the **General Information** screen asks:

- *Will the forthcoming book be published in electronic format only?* If you click Yes, you cannot get an LCCN. An LCCN is for books in print (or eBooks with a print equivalent).
- *Will the book appear at periodic intervals?* Selecting Yes will give you a message that books that appear weekly, monthly, annually, or quarterly are not eligible for an LCCN.

- *Will the book be intended for children or young adults?* A selection of Yes shows another screen asking for Grade Level and Age.
- *Approximate number of pages.* Items under 50 pages, with the exception of genealogies, children's literature, and catalog exhibitions, are not eligible for the PCN Program.
- *Projected publication date.* If you use a date in the past, you receive an error message suggesting you donate your book to the Library of Congress because you cannot get an LCCN.
- *Is the client paying to publish?* Select Yes or No. Note that the system will allow you to continue regardless of your choice. However, your answer here is retained by the system in the event this book is later used by you to apply to the CIP program, which does not allow books subsidized by authors.

Once all the fields are filled-in, click **Next Section**.

Screen two: Contributor Information

Individual is automatically selected but change it to **Organization** if a company name is to be used as the author.

After clicking **Individual** or **Organization**, enter your name (or organization) as it appears on the title page of your book, select **Contributor Type**, and click **Add Contributor**.

As noted in the help text, a **Date of Birth** is requested, but not required (year only). This assists the Library in distinguishing between similar names and omitting it may delay processing.

Add additional contributors if relevant—author, editor, illustrator, translator, complier, and other are the options. Note that the names added in this step are the same as those people you credit when submitting your book for distribution through a publishing portal such as KDP, IngramSpark, and so on.

These are individuals whose contributions were fundamentally necessary and even required to complete the book. A children's book illustrator is an example of someone to include here. Your copyeditor is an example of someone you would not list here.

Click **Add Contributor** for each contributor then click **Next Section** when done.

Screen three: Title Page

Here is where you enter the specific details about your book such as title, subtitle, edition, publisher, and contributors—all of which must match exactly the title page of your book. In fact, if you have a title page in PDF format you can upload it. It's an optional step but doing so may speed the processing of your LCCN application.

There are two important fields to note:

1. If you have purchased ISBNs in the name of your publishing imprint, ignore the instructions under **Publisher Name** which state: *If you are a self-publisher, please enter your name in the field below.* Enter the publishing imprint name you used when buying your ISBN(s). Again, this same name should also be printed at the bottom of your book's title page.
2. If you entered a contributor name in screen two that is different from the title page (for example, you entered Jen Doe on screen two and the title page says Jennifer Doe), you can edit the text box here on screen three so it matches your book's title page.

Screen four: Series & Volume Info

For most books, this page will require only a few clicks.

Series Information, **Yes** or **No**. Enter the **Series Title** and its **Series Volume** if it is part of a series. There is a field for the **ISSN**—International Standard Serial Number—if you have one. But in our world of book publishing this isn't relevant because ISSNs are used to newspapers, journals, magazines, and periodicals—not a series of novels or how-to books. Learn more about ISSNs here: http://breve.link/ryb53.

Volume Information, **Yes** or **No**. Selecting **No**, the screen asks for the **ISBN** for the print edition of your book and its **Format** (hardcover, paperback, spiral bound, and seven other options). These options are similar to the print options available when registering your ISBN using MyIdentifiers. com.

If your book consists of more than one physical volume (you answered **Yes**), the screen expands to ask the volume number (**Vol #**) and **Volume Title** for each volume.

The second part of the **Volume Information** section requires you to answer: *Will the book also be published in electronic format?* If you click **No**, click **Next Section**.

If you select **Yes**, you must enter an ISBN for the eBook. There are ten eBook **Format** types available to be assigned to an ISBN in this section: Adobe PDF, ebook, ebook other, EBK, epub, Kindle Edition, Mobi, Nook Edition, PDF, Other. Make sure you assign the **Format** type for your ISBN that matches what you used at MyIdentifiers.com.

Following my advice from the ISBN chapter, I recommend assigning a single ISBN to an eBook. In this case, choose the **ebook** format for the **Format** field. But if you assigned an ISBN for the **Kindle Edition**, choose that option. If you assigned an addition ISBN to the **epub** (in addition to the ISBN for the Kindle), add that ISBN as well.

If you are not assigning an ISBN to your eBook you have no choice but to answer **No** to the question: *Will the book also be published in electronic format?*

If you are using a free ISBN provided by an aggregator, do not enter that here. This field is for an ISBN that shows you as the publisher and an ISBN from an aggregator will show that aggregator as the publisher.

Screen five: Summary, Contacts, & Additional Info

So far, with very few exceptions, each step in the process for Option 2: Publishers matches Option 1: Authors/Self-Publishers. This screen is notably different and that's because Publisher PCN accounts can have more than one contact managing the LCCN application process.

Book Summary: Enter a description or summary of your book. It must be in English and less than 5,000 characters in length.

Publisher Contacts: you see the name or names entered when you applied for an account along with a button called **Add New Contact**. Enter an additional name if you wish. If you do, this name will show up as an option to select when answering the next three questions:

1. *If the Library of Congress has questions about this submission, who is the appropriate person to contact?*
2. *Who will send a copy of the published book to the Library of Congress?*
3. *Who should receive the email notification with the Library of Congress Control Number (LCCN) for this title?*

After answering the above three questions, the final field is called **Additional Info**. The instructions say *Please use this space to communicate any information you think may be useful in the cataloging process.* This might be if your book has an index, or includes visuals such as photos or illustrations, for example.

However, as of this writing, it is unclear how information like this is used or if it helps a book in some way. If you have such information, note it here, but don't be concerned if you leave it blank. As noted earlier, this is a new system and more clarity may be added in the future.

Screen six: Confirm & Submit

Review the summary of everything you entered and click **Submit** if it is correct. Or return and make corrections.

Final advice: please read

Like any other registration, you will want to be certain about the data you are entering before you begin the process. Being consistent and precise when entering your metadata is absolutely essential because correcting errors can be difficult. Variations in metadata can also reduce or hinder the discoverability of your book. (See **Appendix C** for more advice about managing metadata.)

You will receive a single number for use in all formats you plan to publish (e.g., paperback, eBook, hardcover, audiobook).

Unless you plan to get the P–CIP cataloging block discussed in the next section, you are done for now. Later, after your book is printed, you will mail a complimentary copy of the *best edition* (meaning highest quality) to the LoC for their records. The address information and instructions are in the email you receive confirming your LCCN.

Optional cataloging block: Why, when and how to get a P-CIP cataloging block

Some independent publishers stop after they receive their LCCN. The number links the book to any record that the Library of Congress, other libraries, bibliographic utilities, or book vendors may create.

But if you've come this far, and you believe your book may merit collection by libraries, you should consider investing another $100 or so in having the cataloging block completed by a private company and add it to your book's copyright page. Do *not* attempt to create the cataloging block yourself. The individuals preparing the cataloging blocks are professionals experienced with the categories and classification system used by the LoC, which is different from how a retailer like Amazon might classify a book. The cataloging blocks they create follow the same standards followed by Library of Congress personnel.

The ultimate authority on what becomes part of the cataloging block is the Library of Congress, so you want to choose an individual or firm with demonstrated competence in this regard. These are often former librarians who continue to keep up with changes at the Library of Congress and use this knowledge to ensure your book is categorized for maximum discovery. As a matter of fact, the LoC began implementing changes to the format and content of the cataloging block at the end of 2015 (previously prepared cataloging blocks do not need to be updated). The new format reflects nearly two years of feedback and planning by the LoC and external partners representing key stakeholders such as school, public and academic libraries. Below is an example of the format as prepared for the first edition of *Register Your Book*:

```
Publisher's Cataloging-In-Publication
Data

Names: Wogahn, David.

Title: Register your book : the
essential guide to ISBNs, barcodes,
copyright, and LCCNs / David Wogahn.

Description: Carlsbad, California :
PartnerPress.org, [2016] | Includes
index.

Identifiers: LCCN 2015920990 | ISBN
978-1-944098-05-6 (paperback) | ISBN
978-1-944098-07-0 (hardcover) | ISBN
978-1-944098-06-3 (ebook)

Subjects: LCSH: Publishers and
publishing—Handbooks, manuals, etc.
| Book registration, National—
Handbooks, manuals, etc. | Publishers'
standard book numbers—Handbooks,
```

```
manuals, etc. | Copyright—Handbooks,
manuals, etc.
```
  Classification: LCC Z283 .W64 2016
  (print) | LCC Z283 (ebook) | DDC
  070.5—dc23

Each of these private companies have extensive experience producing P-CIP cataloging blocks. Some of them also submit electronic versions of the records they create to the Online Computer Library Center and/or SkyRiver, both of which are explained in the following sidebar.

- Cassidy Cataloguing: http://breve.link/ryb17
- The Donohue Group: http://breve.link/ryb18
- Five Rainbows: http://breve.link/ryb19
- CIPblock.com: http://breve.link/ryb20

Getting and using your P-CIP cataloging block

Contact one of the firms mentioned above, pay the fee, and complete your application. They will ask you for detailed information about the author and the book. When you receive the cataloging block, you will be instructed to place it, as delivered, on your copyright page. *Do not* reformat it.

MARC Records, OCLC WorldCat, SkyRiver

Another reason to invest in a P-CIP cataloging block is to get your book's information into the online databases used by librarians. This is done through a MARC (MAchine-Readable Cataloging) record, and several of the catalogers listed above will prepare and submit a MARC record in addition to providing you with the P-CIP cataloging block. The MARC record contains additional information not found in the cataloging block that becomes part of your copyright page—information that is useful to librarians.

And how do librarians look up this information? By using WorldCat, a master catalog of more than two billion books held by libraries around the world. (You can learn more about WorldCat by visiting the Online Computer Library Center website, the administrator of WorldCat: OCLC.org.)

Another, although much smaller, database used by some libraries is called SkyRiver, part of Innovative Interfaces Inc. Like an investment in Library of Congress cataloging itself, ensuring your book is submitted to SkyRiver may or may not be of benefit. A few of the catalogers mentioned above also submit MARC records to SkyRiver, so look for that service (in addition to WorldCat) if you feel it may benefit your book. You can learn more about SkyRiver by visiting http://breve.link/ryb21.

6

The Bare Minimum

————————

A nyone can publish a book. As I said at the out-
set, not every book needs an ISBN, barcode,
copyright filing, or a Library of Congress Control Number. But to maximize book sales and protect your investment, it helps if you keep the following in mind:

1. If you obtain an ISBN, complete the assignment
   process. You want your book listed in as many
   databases as possible.
2. Be consistent in how you describe your book
   when filling out forms and keep track of where
   you submit this information. If you make changes
   later, go back and update *all* the locations that
   have information about your book.
3. Wherever you have a chance to enter book
   metadata—stores, industry databases, and so

forth—complete all available fields. (See **Appen-dix C** for more advice on managing metadata.)

Beyond these minimal guidelines, your use of the advice in *Register Your Book* depends greatly on your book and your goals. Also, be sure to read the next two appendices—**Timing and Timelines** and **Maximizing SEO Benefits**.

Two Final Things

Would you mind leaving a few words about this book in a review on Amazon, Goodreads, or wherever you bought it? It doesn't have to be long or detailed—the main thing is to share your opinion. This helps other readers decide if my book might be valuable to them.

Thanks, I really appreciate it.

Once again, each time I release a book or training resource I offer everyone on my mailing list advance notice about an exclusive launch offer. If you'd like to get notified, please visit DavidWogahn.com/join to sign-up or subscribe to one of the free resources at AuthorImprints.com.

You'll be a member of my low-volume mailing list and can unsubscribe anytime. Readers enjoy insightful interviews and high-value articles about book marketing and publishing.

Visit DavidWogahn.com/join.

Also by David Wogahn

Learn more at
DavidWogahn.com/brc

Learn more at
DavidWogahn.com/mpi

Learn more at
DavidWogahn.com/bryp

Appendix A
Timing and Timelines

I f you are like many new publishers, you begin thinking about book production and distribution *after* you have written your book. There is nothing wrong with this. Just keep in mind that there is a specific sequence to "registering your book" and that certain optional steps—namely, securing a P–CIP cataloging block—can take time.

Here are the steps, in priority order, and the general timeframes associated with each of the three major book registration activities. Refer to the noted chapter for more details, including costs and additional requirements.

Note that not every step will apply to every book. All of these are optional, and the time to complete each step is subject to change at any time.

Publisher's Steps:	Purchase ISBN(s) if you plan to use your own imprint name
See Chapter:	2
Time to Complete:	Immediate
Note:	You must have an ISBN in the name of your publishing imprint if you plan to apply for a Library of Congress Control Number (LCCN). Free ISBNs are not accepted.
Publisher's Steps:	Apply to the Library of Congress Preassigned Control Number (PCN) program (Author/Self-Publisher or Publisher)
See Chapter:	5
Time to Complete:	1 to 2 weeks (stated timing, but can be less)
Note:	• If you choose to apply for a Publisher account, this is the first of two steps for acquiring an LCCN • Those who choose the Author/Self-Publisher PCN account will apply for a LCCN at the same time

Publisher's Steps:	Assign ISBN(s) to book by submitting ISBN assignment in MyIdentifiers
See Chapter:	2
Time to Complete:	Immediate
Note:	Allow days, if not weeks, for industry databases to receive ISBN details. However, you can publish your book at any time.
Publisher's Steps:	Apply for an LCCN. (Applies only to those who applied for a PCN Publisher account.)
See Chapter:	5
Time to Complete:	1 to 2 weeks (stated timing, but can be less)
Note:	Assuming your PCN application for a Publisher account is approved
Publisher's Steps:	Order a P-CIP cataloging block
See Chapter:	5
Time to Complete:	1 to 2 weeks (may be less)
Note:	An optional investment for nonfiction and unimportant for fiction

Publisher's Steps:	Apply for copyright registration
See Chapter:	4
Time to Complete:	Immediate (however, processing takes months)
Note:	Initiated once the book is final. If you preregistered, you still need to file for registration when your book is published.
Publisher's Steps:	Mail a copy of the finished book to the Library of Congress
See Chapter:	5
Time to Complete:	Immediate
Note:	Assuming you received an LCCN

Appendix B
Maximizing SEO Benefits

Optimizing metadata and its importance for search engines

The phrase "search engine optimization" (SEO) is practically synonymous with Google and positioning one's website to show up on the first page of results when someone searches for a specific word or phrase. What does this have to do with authors and publishers? The reality is that there are lots and lots of search engines, including the search engines that help you find products in online stores, the largest of which is Amazon.

> From 2015 to 2018, Amazon surpassed Google for product searches. During this time period, Amazon's share of searches

grew from 46% to 54% and Google decline from 54% to 46%.[11]

Amazon dwarfs Google when it comes to product search

It turns out that there are many things an author can control to help their book be more visible on Amazon, and most of these techniques can be applied to other bookstores, social networks, and industry databases, not to mention traditional search engines like Google and Bing. Authors achieve this by creating and optimizing metadata—information that describes their book and their websites that is (in many cases) invisible to us humans but visible to software programs. An ISBN is one of these metadata elements.

There are two key facts about SEO benefits to keep in mind:

1. SEO for books is alive and well. Its importance may have diminished for some Internet marketers,[12] but every book listing must be optimized just like every website page must be optimized.
2. Secondly, your book listing by any search engine—most especially Amazon's—is paramount. Even if the buyer does their shopping on

Barnes & Noble, Kobo, or the Apple iBook store, your book must be *discoverable*.

Optimizing your book's listing for search is just one of the many marketing tactics you should employ. You still need to promote your book. But when people do come looking for your book or a book on your subject, a book will be far more likely to appear in search results if the book's metadata has been optimized.

Complete your ISBN record for maximum search benefits

Whether you are using an ISBN because you are required to, or simply out of preference, your investment will be that much more valuable if you complete your book's record in the database. Furthermore, the earlier you can complete it, the sooner it will show up in industry databases (more on this below).

Nielsen, the parent company of Bowker, has presented research stating that when publishers submit a cover, book description, author bio, and book reviews, *average sales rise by 55% in comparison to books with records that have none of these elements.*[13]

Part of the credit goes to distribution of your ISBN information to a range of users. According to Bowker, information about your book will be available to:

- 3,000 subscribers of the *Books In Print* and *Global Books* database.
- 1,800 library customers, including the New York Public Library, Harvard University Library, and the British Library.
- 5,000 libraries and branch locations.
- Retail customers, including Barnes & Noble, Follett (college bookstores), and independent bookstores.
- School systems.
- Pubnet.org and PubEasy.com, e-commerce systems for the book industry.

Whether you buy the ISBN yourself or receive one assigned by an author services company (Author Solutions, Lulu, Outskirts Press, etc.), you'll want to make sure your book's information is entered in the official records in order to maximize its discoverability.

Spotlighting the benefits of early and complete ISBN record submission

AuthorImprints was recently hired to manage a high-profile book project that required establishing the imprint and managing the publishing process, including all the registration steps outlined in this book. This was a typical independent publishing scenario. It was this publisher's first book, and we were managing a myriad of details, including delays assembling metadata. Most notably, we lacked a PDF of the book itself, which prevented us from finalizing all the details until just a few weeks before its release. (Second edition note: Bowker no longer asks publishers to upload a PDF when registering an ISBN.)

We submitted all the relevant details to our MyIdentifiers account for each ISBN about seven weeks prior to the release date. Because most of our distribution was through online stores, I had a process in place to regularly search for the title and ISBN using Google and Bing. Surprisingly, I came across a listing for the hardcover edition in the online store for the large South Florida bookstore group, Books and Books.

Up until this point the only public listings of the hardcover ISBN were through MyIdentifiers and Amazon. And since Amazon isn't in the business of notifying, much less supplying, competitors with information about new books, we can only assume the BooksandBooks.com listing came via Bowker's MyIdentifiers data feed. The upshot was that we were able to contact the store and arrange a book event for the author.

It didn't end there. Before the book was even released, we had orders from a wholesaler that serves libraries and schools. They contacted us because they found the book via Bowker's *Books In Print* database.

Using an ISBN and submitting the assignment as early as feasible pays off.

Internet search and the ISBN

Internet search has evolved in the direction of assigning greater importance to structured data and unique identifiers such as the ISBN. This has garnered support from key search engines such as Google, Bing, Yahoo, and Yandex. Google Knowledge Graph (still a work in progress) is an example of this direction and the ISBN plays a central role in returning relevant search results for queries involving books.

The goal of these efforts is to provide authoritative search results rather than results dominated by a handful of companies with their own commercial interests. As Internet search becomes ever more important, there is reason to believe we can expect the ISBN to become a definitive signal. Industry standard identifiers like the ISBN make this possible.

Appendix C

How to Manage Metadata: Seven Habits for Success

Metadata is the wrapper of information that surrounds and describes our books, our company, and even us as publishers or authors. In *Register Your Book*, the metadata we discussed is all the information we enter during the registration process at MyIdentifiers.com, Copyright.gov, and LoC.gov. But metadata also includes things like categories, keywords, descriptions, and extends further to include information about the author and his or her platform.

How is your metadata prepared and maintained?

Your approach can be, and needs to be, fundamental. It begins with the right work habits and taking ownership of the process.

So with apologies to Stephen Covey, here are the seven habits of smart metadata managers.

1. Record it.

This seems to be the number one problem for new and occasional publishers. Recording and referencing information about your book(s) and yourself in a standard way is essential, but it's also challenging because the information is used in so many places and in so many different ways. Stores, websites, and marketing tools all differ in terms of what they ask for or permit.

Consider the book category field. Some stores, such as Amazon, maintain their own category lists while others use the Book Industry Standards and Communications (BISAC) subject headings. The only way to keep your metadata consistent is to record it and use these records as your source for new applications or changes.

A simple spreadsheet or document file will suffice for cost-effective record keeping. You might also keep a record of information that never changes (ISBNs, for instance) in your contact management system.

2. Make it accurate.

That's another way of saying be precise. For instance, if your book title includes a hyphenated word, did you use a hyphen in that word when you listed the book in online stores? What about in written materials such as press releases?

3. Make it consistent.

This goes hand-in-hand with being accurate. Think about the various metadata elements that describe your book—title, description, author name, series name (if applicable), and so on. This should be the same everywhere, including in the ISBN record, in online store listings, in websites, in social media profiles, within the book, and in promotional material.

4. Make it timely.

Release your metadata publicly as soon as it is accurate, especially your ISBN metadata. The key here is careful planning. Savvy publishers don't rush to market. They pick a realistic publication date in the future and manage to that date. As decisions are made, they lock in data and put it online as soon as possible so it can be indexed by search engines. They also promptly update the information if it changes.

5. Disseminate it.

Key destinations for metadata include social cataloging sites such as Goodreads and LibraryThing, author and publisher websites, and leading social media sites such as Facebook, Twitter, and LinkedIn, as well as major online book retailers.

6. Optimize it.

Optimizing metadata is the process of adapting your standard metadata so that it will work better with a specific online service. For books, the opportunity to optimize most commonly involves subject categories and search terms for online stores. As noted, the category field may, and often does, differ among online platforms, including Amazon KDP (Kindle and KDP Print), Barnes & Noble, Kobo, MyIdentifiers, and more. There are additional optimization opportunities on sites such as Twitter, Facebook, and LinkedIn.

7. Maintain it.

Because things change, managing metadata is not a set-and-forget activity. Publishing a new book, changing a book category or keywords to reach new readers, replacing a profile picture, rephrasing a book description to reflect review feedback—all these require circling back to refresh your metadata.

Resources

Where to buy ISBNs

The issuance of ISBNs is managed on a country-by-country basis by more than 160 ISBN agencies worldwide. Below are the sources for countries where English is the dominant or de facto language. To look up an agency for a country not listed below, visit the International ISBN Agency website: http://breve.link/ryb22.

Again, acquire ISBNs from the country where the publisher is located.

- Australia (Thorpe-Bowker): http://breve.link/ryb23
- Canada, English (Library and Archives Canada): http://breve.link/ryb24
- Canada, French (Library and Archives Canada): http://breve.link/ryb25
- New Zealand (National Library of New Zealand): http://breve.link/ryb26

- United Kingdom and Ireland (Nielsen UK ISBN Agency): http://breve.link/ryb27
- United States and U.S. territories (R.R.Bowker/ MyIdentifiers.com): http://breve.link/ryb28

Converting ISBNs

Sometimes it is necessary to convert an ISBN between the ISBN-13 and ISBN-10 format, such as when you want to create a short link to your book on Amazon (described below). Converting an ISBN between these two formats is easily done using this free tool: http://breve.link/ryb29.

By the way, even though the numbers look similar, do not attempt to edit the number yourself. The last digit of every ISBN is a check digit, a mathematically calculated number based on the preceding 12 digits (or nine for the older ISBN-10).

How to create short links to your book or eBook

Once your book is published, you'll of course want to tell everyone about it. Emailing a long URL isn't attractive or even practical if you want to print it on your business card. That's where creating short links come in. There are several ways you can do this, but I'm going to outline the most straightforward approach for three of the major U.S. stores.

First, be sure you have:

- Both the long (ISBN-13) and short (ISBN-10) ISBN. You can use the ISBN converter tool noted above if you have only one of these numbers. Do not simply drop the first three numbers (978) to create the ISBN-10.
- For Amazon Kindle eBooks, you need your eBook's ASIN. You can find it in the **Product Details** information on your book's sales page on Amazon, as illustrated below.
- For eBooks sold on BarnesandNoble.com, the number to use is labeled ISBN-13. (Note that Barnes & Noble assigns their own number if you upload your eBook to their store via Barnes & Noble Press. Like Amazon, they ignore your eBook's ISBN, if you assign one.) Again, look it up on BarnesandNoble.com based on the screen shot that follows.

Amazon Kindle eBooks

Replace the bolded number with your ASIN.

https://amzn.com/**B01BX7Q02K**/

Product details

File Size: 2030 KB
Print Length: 178 pages
Simultaneous Device Usage: Unlimited
Publisher: PartnerPress; 2 edition (March 17, 2016)
Publication Date: March 17, 2016
Sold by: Amazon.com Services LLC
Language: English
ASIN: B01BX7Q02K
Text-to-Speech: Enabled ⌄
X-Ray:
Enabled ⌄
Word Wise: Enabled
Lending: Enabled
Enhanced Typesetting: Enabled ⌄

Amazon print books

Amazon uses the ISBN-10 number for print books rather than the ASIN. Replace the bolded number with your ISBN-10 number.

https://amzn.com/**1944098119**

Product details

Series: Countdown to Book Launch (Book 2)
Paperback: 176 pages
Publisher: PartnerPress (July 10, 2019)
Language: English
ISBN-10: 1944098119
ISBN-13: 978-1944098117
Product Dimensions: 5.2 x 0.4 x 8 inches

Barnes & Noble Nook eBooks

Find your book's identifier on your book's product listing page and replace it in the bolded example here:

http://www.bn.com/s/**2940163646074**

Product Details

BN ID:	2940163646074
Publisher:	PartnerPress.org
Publication date:	10/24/2019
Series:	Countdown to Book Launch
Sold by:	Draft2Digital
Format:	NOOK Book
File size:	2 MB

Barnes & Noble print books

Barnes & Noble differs from Amazon in that they use the longer ISBN-13 rather than ISBN-10 for print books. Replace the bolded ISBN-13 in the example here with your ISBN-13:

http://www.bn.com/s/**9780979439124**.

Apple Books (eBooks only)

You cannot send someone a link to buy a book from Apple Books, but you can link to what is called an

Apple Books **Preview**. Place the ISBN-13 for your eBook at the end of the URL, immediately following the letters **isbn** (all lower case), like this:

https://books.apple.com/us/book/
isbn**9781948025010**.

eBook ISBN requirements by distributor and store

This is a quick guide to the ISBN requirements for major eBook stores and eBook distributors (also known as aggregators) that accept eBooks from indie publishers. As stated earlier, it is up to the distributor or retailer whether an ISBN is required. All print books sold in stores must have an ISBN. For more detail about eBook aggregators, including how and when to choose one, please read my annual round-up of eBook aggregators: http://breve.link/ryb55.

eBook Distributor or Store	Requires ISBN?
Amazon Kindle	Not required
Apple Books	Not required
Barnes & Noble Nook	Not required
Kobo Books	Not required
Google Play Books	Not required

eBook Distributor or Store	Requires ISBN?
Bookbaby	Required or buy for $29*
Draft2Digital	Required or provided free
EBookIt	Required or provided free
eBookPartnership	Required or provided free
Feiyr	Required or provided free
IngramSpark	Required or buy for $85*
PublishDrive	Not required or provided free
PublishGreen	Required or provided free
Smashwords	Required or provided free
Streetlib	Required or provided free
XinXii	Provided free or fee for nonfiction; free for fiction

* The Bookbaby ISBN will show them as the publisher. Ingram-Spark is an authorized reseller so your publishing imprint will show as the publisher.

Deciphering an ISBN

Today's ISBN was originally called a Standard Book Numbering code. It dates back to 1965, when it was developed by a professor of statistics at Trinity College in Dublin, Ireland, for the U.K. bookseller WHSmith. The format was modified on January 1, 2007, to accommodate the growth of books and to comply with international standards. Today, all ISBNs begin with 978 or the new prefix, 979.

When you understand the format, you can see why it is helpful for publishers to own a block of numbers rather than acquire them as needed. The images below illustrate this perfectly.

If you buy 10 ISBNs from MyIdentifiers.com, your publisher number is in positions six to eleven, shown here as 348839:

If you buy 100 ISBNs from MyIdentifiers.com, your publisher number is in positions six to ten, shown here as 44098:

Further reading about ISBNs

"Book numbering: the importance of the ISBN," Philip Bradley. http://breve.link/ryb31

The Metadata Handbook, Renée Register and Thad McIlroy (DataCurate, Second Edition, March 2015)

"Nielsen Book UK Study: The Importance of Metadata for Discoverability and Sales," Nielsen Book Services. Andre Breedt, revised 2016. http://breve.link/ryb32

"BISG Policy Statement POL-1101: Best Practices for Identifying Digital Products," Book Industry Study Group. Revised February 25, 2013. http://breve.link/ryb33

Glossary

Acid-Free Paper. Paper that has a neutral or basic pH (7 or slightly higher). Books using acid-free paper can be preserved for a longer time period than those that are not printed on acid-free paper.

Aggregator. An eBook aggregator receives an eBook and distributes that file to more than one online retailer (e.g., Amazon, Apple, Barnes & Noble). They make money by charging fees or keeping a percentage of sales. Services and capabilities vary, as do the online stores each eBook aggregator will service. eBook aggregators typically specialize in markets, such as self-publishers (authors) vs. traditional publishers.

ARC, Advance Reading (or Review) Copy. A book that is provided to readers in advance of the publication date for the purpose of soliciting a review, endorsement, or some other contribution to the book. Usually books sent out for this purpose are marked as such with wording clearly indicating it is an Advance Reading Copy.

ASIN, Amazon Standard Identification Number. A proprietary 10-digit identification number that Amazon assigns to every product it sells. Keep in mind it is not necessarily unique because it can vary by Amazon store (U.K., Germany, Japan, etc.). For print books with an ISBN-10 number—those books with an ISBN assigned prior to January 1, 2007—the ASIN and ISBN are the same.

Barcode. A barcode is a machine-readable series of parallel lines that represent a sequence of numbers. Every physical book sold at retail must have an ISBN and corresponding barcode. The Universal Product Code (UPC) is also represented by a barcode, and it is not uncommon to see both ISBN and UPC numbers and barcodes in a single block on a book cover. But in practice, the UPC code is relevant only for those publishers who sell their physical books in non-bookstore locations such as supermarkets, drug stores and mass-merchant retailers.

BISG, Book Industry Study Group. The U.S. trade association that sets polices and standards related to books and publishing, including recommendations for ISBN usage.

Bowker or R.R. Bowker. A private company authorized by the International ISBN Agency to issue ISBNs to publishers located in the United States and U.S. territories. If you want the name of your publishing company to be listed as the publisher of your book, you need to buy your ISBN from Bowker or an authorized reseller. If you are unsure if the reseller is authorized, you should check with Bowker. ISBNs are purchased from MyIdentifiers.com and you can find the official (U.S.) Bowker website at http://breve.link/ryb34.

Cataloging Block. A bibliographic record that appears printed on the verso of the book's title page, commonly referred to as the copyright page. It is an abbreviated version of the machine-readable cataloging (or MARC) record that resides in the Library of Congress's database and which is distributed to libraries and book vendors. The full MARC version contains additional information such as codes that indicate the language in which the book is written, the date when the book was cataloged, etc.

Check Digit. The last number at the end of both the ISBN-10 and ISBN-13 is the check digit. Check digits are computed by applying a mathematical formula to the preceding nine or twelve numbers depending on whether it is an ISBN-10 or ISBN-13, respectively. The purpose is to identify incorrectly entered numbers, which of course won't compute the correct check digit.

Data Block. See *Cataloging Block.*

DRM, Digital Rights Management. DRM is a form of copy protection applied by software or retailers to help prevent unauthorized sharing of eBooks. The decision whether to protect an eBook by applying DRM is up to the publisher, not the retailer.

Discovery. A term used in book publishing to describe the process of helping readers find books in which they may be interested. This is especially important in an increasingly online book-buying world where searching online is replacing a visit to the local bookstore. Discovery begins with accurate and detailed metadata, and extends to placing a book in all the places a prospective reader might come across it, regardless of whether they thought they might want to read it. This includes stores, search engines, key influencers, social media networks, and the media.

Distributor. In print book distribution, a distributor has an exclusive agreement with a book publisher to sell the publisher's books to retailers, including Amazon. They also use book wholesalers, such as Ingram, to help them get books to retailers. Because a distributor only makes money when its publishers sell books, it carefully chooses its publishers based on the type and number of titles a publisher has published and their sales history. Also see **Wholesaler.**

EPUB. An international, open-source file format for eBooks. The official governing body is the International Digital Publishing Forum (IDPF.org). Also see **Mobi.**

Imprint. An imprint is like a brand name for a line of books from a publisher. For small publishers, it is often the same name as the name of the publisher, yet it is possible for a publisher to have multiple imprints. Like any brand name, each imprint is chosen to create meaning and establish a reputation in the mind of the consumer. It isn't necessarily a formal entity, like a corporation or LLC, but it can be. In publishing, the name of the imprint is listed on the copyright page and used when you purchase and assign ISBNs, to name two common applications.

ISSN, International Standard Serial Number. Similar to an ISBN in that it refers to a print and/or electronic publication, the ISSN is specifically for periodical publications such as newspapers and magazines.

Metadata. In layman's terms, metadata can be defined as information about information. Metadata for books refers to everything from the title, author name, and description to the size, file type, or weight—all the details about a book that are included in databases and search engines. For many small or independent publishers, all you need to know is that the information you enter into MyIdentifiers.com (if you use an ISBN) and the self-service distribution pages for KDP, Nook Press, Apple Books, etc., is metadata.

Mobi. A file format not unlike EPUB in that it is used to display an eBook. It was originally developed in 2000 by the French firm Mobipocket SA, which was acquired by Amazon in 2005. Without getting into the technical details about Amazon's other eBook file formats, it is important to note that if you have the Mobi version of your eBook, you can email it to anyone and they can read it using a free Amazon Kindle app. Just keep in mind that to digitally protect the file (using DRM), you need to sell it via Amazon's Kindle store.

MyIdentifiers.com. See *Bowker.*

ONIX, ONline Information eXchange. A data format standard for tracking and exchanging information about books that includes only those books that have ISBNs. It is a way to move data between various members of the supply chain: from publisher to retailer, and everyone in between.

R.R. Bowker: See *Bowker.*

SEO, Search Engine Optimization. SEO is the process of influencing the discovery of information or metadata within a particular search engine. Every search engine, including those used by online retailers like Amazon, use proprietary and usually unpublished algorithms to determine what someone sees when they perform a search. Each unit—a web page or book's page in an online store, for example—contains non-visible, descriptive information, called Metadata. This metadata is evaluated by a search engine's algorithms to determine its relevance to the entered search. The goal for the person doing the search is to find what they are looking for, while the goal of the search engine is to show the result deemed most relevant by the search engine.

Your goal, as the publisher or author, is to optimize your book's metadata in such a way that it appears among the results for relevant search words.

UPC, Universal Product Code. A physical stock tracking number and associated barcode to identify products. It is widely used in the major English-speaking countries and relates to books only in certain circumstances. Also see *Barcode.* This is generally not something the average small publisher needs to be concerned with.

URL, Uniform Resource Locator. A URL is a string of characters that serves as the address to reach some kind of resource on the Internet. Most often the term is associated with a web page resource that begins with HTTP.The URL for a particular page is in the address bar of the web browser used to navigate the Internet.

Wholesaler. A wholesaler is a middleman between the publisher—or publisher's representative such as a distributor—and a retailer. Ingram is the largest book wholesaler now that Baker & Taylor has closed its retail wholesale business (July 2019). Retailers that wish to order books do so via Ingram so it is imperative that publishers have their books listed in the Ingram catalog. This happens automatically if a publisher uses IngramSpark, or if you select Expanded Distribution in KDP Print. Also see *Distributor.*

WorldCat. A database of book records that itemizes the collections of 72,000 libraries in 170 countries and territories that participate in the Online Computer Library Center (OCLC) global cooperative.

Notes

1. *Self-Publishing in the United States,* 2012-2017 (Bowker, 2018). http://breve.link/ryb43.

2. See this comparison of e-book formats for a complete list. http://breve.link/ryb36.

3. For a humorous look at the frustration with those that use the term eISBN, see Laura Dawson's presentation "Every time you say eISBN a Kitten Bleeds." http://breve.link/ryb37.

4. "BISG Policy Statement POL-1101: Best Practices for Identifying Digital Products," Book Industry Study Group. Revised February 25, 2013. http://breve.link/ryb38.

5. 2013 eBook Self-Publisher Research Survey Results, available on Slideshare.net. http://breve.link/ryb39.

6. Bowker does not specifically define "typos" or what number of corrections you can make before you need to issue a different ISBN. http://breve.link/ryb40.

7. Apple iBooks FAQ. http://breve.link/ryb41.

8. "BISG Policy Statement POL-1101: Best Practices for Identifying Digital Products," Book Industry Study Group. Revised February 25, 2013. http://breve.link/ryb42.

9. *Self-Publishing in the United States,* 2012-2017 (Bowker, 2018). http://breve.link/ryb43.

10. Schwabach, Aaron (Jan 15, 2014). *Internet and the Law: Technology, Society, and Compromises.* ABC-CLIO. p. 149. ISBN 9781610693509. http://breve.link/ryb45.

11. Jumpshot data report, Q21, 2018.

12. Sean Jackson's article on Copyblogger, "SEO is Dead: Long Live OC/DC," clarifies why "SEO" as a term is evolving. http://breve.link/ryb47.

13. Nielsen Book's White Paper: The Link Between Metadata and Sales. http://breve.link/ryb48.

Acknowledgments

The beloved children's classic *If You Give a Mouse a Cookie* describes the origin of this book—the initial source of encouragement to undertake this effort.

It began with a blog post in 2012 on the topic of ISBNs for eBooks. At the time there was significant confusion among indie publishers (and even book industry companies) about the topic and I decided to boil it down to a simple five-point FAQ. This led to a blog post on the mythical *eISBN*—a post that garnered a link from Wikipedia for its authenticity—and a post to clarify the four ISBN choices (since reduced to three) offered by Amazon's CreateSpace (now KDP Print).

Collectively, these posts have attracted more than 200 comments and countless readers. So it is only appropriate that I begin here with a note of appreciation to those commenters and readers. Without their keen interest, I would never have thought there was a market for such a book.

There is no single entity that governs all aspects of what I call *book registration*. Once I had the book's audience and key topics defined, it was a matter of vetting the information with subject matter experts. **Judith Appelbaum, Laura Dawson, Karla Olson, Terry Tegnazian,** and **Valerie Nemeth** all made meaningful contributions that helped fine-tune the clarity and accuracy of the information found in the book.

I imagine many authors experience some form of indecision or have a need for trusted advice. **Julia and Jared Drake, Leslie Lehr, Peter Lichtgarn,** and **Teri Rider:** Thank you for finding the time to share your wise counsel and for your encouragement.

And finally, all this would not be possible if it wasn't for **Melissa**'s support. You are always there to provide the unvarnished feedback that I need to hear. I am forever grateful to you.

About the Author

D avid Wogahn is a LinkedIn Learning author and the author of five books including *My Publishing Imprint* and *The Book Reviewer Yellow Pages*.

The content of his books draws from his in-depth experience as president of the award-winning author-services company AuthorImprints.com. AuthorImprints.com has helped more than 125 authors professionally self-publish books using their own publishing imprint.

During David's 30 years in publishing and online media, he has worked for the *Los Angeles Times*, the Los Angeles Olympic Organizing Committee, and was co-founder of the first online publisher of sports team branded websites known today as the CBS College Sports Network.

He is a frequent speaker and trainer, including presentations for the Independent Book Publishers Association, the Alliance of Independent Authors (ALLi), the Independent Writers of

Southern California, and the Santa Barbara Writers Conference.

Contact David by visiting DavidWogahn.com or AuthorImprints.com.